AFRICAN PROVERBS

Gerd de Ley

AFRICAN PROVERBS

Gerd de Ley

Some translations are made by
David Potter

HIPPOCRENE BOOKS, INC.
New York

ISBN 0-7818-0691-7

For information, address:
HIPPOCRENE BOOKS, INC.
171 Madison Avenue
New York, NY 10016

Printed in the United States of America

Dedicated to Mireille Cottenjé
whose love for Africa
was very inspiring.

INTRODUCTION

Africa is often referred to as "The Dark Continent"—in the sense that little is generally known about the culture of the African nations, tribes, and people. Often, much of what we hear about such countries is how they were colonized or decolonized or how civil war was waged, rather than anything about the underlying ethos of the countries and people, themselves.

The many nations of Africa differ greatly from one another, and proverbs on such topics as skin hue and religion help to point out these unique differences. Proverbs on slavery reflect a historical time of anguish, struggle, and of establishing a cultural identity. Furthermore, proverbs about crocodiles, snakes, elephants and other animals tell a great deal about human nature on a more universal level. These are just a handful of the topics included in this extensive volume of African proverbs.

For more than twenty years I have been collecting and translating proverbs from around the world. They reveal much about the wisdom, humor, and character of other countries and peoples. I have also discovered, as you will, that proverbs are cosmopolites, and that every exception proves the rule.

I hope that this collection of African proverbs will lend insight into the many and varied aspects of this Continent, revealing the rich culture it had—and, indeed, still enjoys. (Perhaps, then, Africa is not such a "dark" place after all?)

I wish you well on your tour of Africa . . .

Gerd de Ley

HOW TO USE THIS BOOK

These proverbs are classified according to key words. In the case of most proverbs, the reader can find the name of the country, province or even the tribe that is the source of a particular proverb. However, in some cases, the source could not be found, and has thus been left blank. Such cases may be classified simply as "general"—that is, the proverb is found to be derived from more than one country or from more than one tribe.

ABOUT PROVERBS

Proverbs are the palm-oil with which words are eaten.   IBO

An old woman is always uneasy when dry bones are
    mentioned in a proverb.   CHINUA ACHEBE

A proverb is to speech what salt is to food.   ETHIOPIA

A proverb is the horse of conversation: when the
    conversation lags, a proverb will revive it.   YORUBA

When the occasion arises, there is a proverb to suit it.   OJI

Proverbs are the daughters of experience.   RWANDA BURUNDI

When the fool is told a proverb, its meaning has to be
    explained to him.   ASHANTI

He who uses proverbs, gets what he wants.   ZIMBABWE

When a poor man makes a proverb it does not spread
    abroad.   ASHANTI

A wise man who knows proverbs reconciles difficulties.   YORUBA

A

ABSENCE

Absence makes the heart forget.   KENYA

ABUNDANCE

Abundance in the world becomes great with good faith.   MOROCCO

Abundance does not spread, famine does.   ZULU

Abundance will make cotton pull a stone.   HAUSA

Superabundance is not far from want.   NIGERIA

ABUSE

Abuses are the result of seeing one another too often.   SWAHILI

ACCIDENT

An accident is not like an expected result.   YORUBA

ACCOMPLISHMENT

Whatever accomplishment you boast of in the world,
    there is someone better than you.   HAUSA

ADULTERY

Adultery is like dung; one goes far to do it.   BEMBA

The tears of the adulteress are ever ready to be shed.   EGYPT

ADVICE

Advise and counsel him; if he does not listen,
    let adversity teach him.   ETHIOPIA

Advice is a stranger; if he's welcome he stays for the night;
    if not, he leaves the same day.   MALAGASY

AFFECTION

Mutual affection is when each gives his share.   IVORY COAST

AFFLICTION

After every affliction there is enjoyment.   MOROCCO

Africa

The African race is like an Indian rubber ball; the harder you
dash it to the ground, the higher it will rise.   ‘   BANTU

Age

When one's peers in age die it is a warning to oneself.   SENEGAL

Agreement

An agreement is a kind of debt.   MOROCCO

Ahead

The man who goes ahead stumbles that the man who follows
may have his wits about him.   BONDEI

The man ahead does not drink fouled water.   BONDEI

Aim

Taking aim for too long can ruin your eyes.   IVORY COAST

Aiming isn't hitting.   SWAHILI

Before firing, you must take aim.   NIGERIA

Alcoholic

One hundred alcoholics are better than one gambler.   TUNISIA

Allah (God)

People in trouble remember Allah.   HAUSA

Allah preserve us from 'If only I'd known!'   HAUSA

Alone

One who runs alone cannot be outrun by another.   ETHIOPIA

Ambition

Ambition begets troubles.   SENEGAL

A man with too much ambition cannot sleep in peace.   BAGUIRMI

He who desires to attain things must pass through
many nights.   TUNISIA

Ambush

You cannot avoid what lies in ambush for you.   OVAMBO

4

ANCESTORS

Ancestors, ancestors guide me to whatever I'm looking for, whatever it may be.   ETHIOPIA

ANGEL

When the angels appear, the devils run away.   EGYPT

Each person lives with his own guardian angel.   IBO

ANGER

Anger without power is a ready blow.   EGYPT

To spend the night in anger is better than to spend it repenting.   SENEGAL

The anger of a woman is mighty and the devil's trickery weak.   TUNISIA

ANIMAL

A large animal is nice but difficult to feed.   HAUSA

When an animal is going to bite you, it does not show its teeth.   ASHANTI

An animal that has just escaped from a trap fears a bent stick.   ANNANG

The flesh of a young animal tastes flat.   CONGO

If a bush is surrounded, the animals in it are easily killed.   YORUBA

Better to be watched by a wild animal than a nosey man.   BERBER

ANT

If they are offered winged ants, people will eat them.

He who cannot pick up an ant, and wants to pick up an elephant will some day see his folly.   YORUBA

The little ant at its hole is full of courage.   BEMBA

He who runs from the white ant may stumble upon the stinging ant.   NIGERIA

Ants can attack with a grain of rice.   MALAGASY

Caution is not cowardice; even the ants march armed.   UGANDA

ANTELOPE

Two small antelopes can beat one big one.   ASHANTI

5

Anxiety

Anxiety will not let you to die of hunger.

Approach

When someone is already approaching, there is no need
to say: 'Come here.'   Ashanti

Arm

The arms are not taken away by a woman's sexual organs.   Ovambo

Army

An army is driven back by courage and not by insults,
however many.   Ashanti

When an army suffers defeat, a horn is not blown in
its honor.   Ashanti

Arrow

The arrow you dropped will be collected by someone else. Ovambo

When you see an arrow that is not going to miss you, throw
out your chest and meet it head on.   Congo

Artist

In crooked wood one recognizes the artist.   Ewe

Ashes

Ashes will always blow back into the face of the thrower. Yoruba

The glow soon becomes ashes.   Egypt

Ask

Don't ask me where I am going but where I have come from.

Ass

He who lives with an ass, sounds like an ass.   Ethiopia

A little nod is enough for the wise man; an ass needs a fist. Morocco

Assistance

Assistance conquers a lion.   Morocco

Bakuba painted mask with hood decorated with cowrie shells and beads, Kasai region. Belgian Congo. Wood. Tervueren, Musée Royal du Congo Belge.

ATTACHMENT

Strong attachment is difficult—it makes one mad or kills.   MOROCCO

ATTIC

He who lives in the attic knows where the roof leaks.   NIGERIA

ATTRACTIVE

An attractive person cannot be without blemish—if he does
    not steal he bewitches.   ZAMBIA

AUNT

A hundred aunts is not the same as one mother.   SIERRA LEONE

AUTHORITY

Authority does not depend on age.   OVAMBO

He who has no authority will not have ceremonial drums.   FULANI

AVARICE

Avarice destroys what the avaricious gathers.   BOTSWANA

Avarice is the root of all evil.   SWAHILI

AXE

An axe with a loose head is the bane of a man up a tree.   HAUSA

An axe for wax will not cut rock.   FULANI

An axe is sharp on soft wood.   OVAMBO

An axe without a handle does not cut firewood.   SWAHILI

Even a small axe is better than striking with a stick.   OVAMBO

He who continually uses an axe, must keep it sharp.   HAUSA

The axe forgets but the cut log does not.   SHONA

B

BABY

When the baby grows, the crying changes. ANNANG

BACK

A back does not break from bending. EGYPT

BAD LUCK

What is bad luck for one man is good luck for another. ASHANTI

BALD

Baldness is a thing of dignity. JABO

When a single hair has fallen from your head, you are not
yet bald. SIERRA LEONE

The bald woman boasts of her sister's hair. TUNISIA

A bald-headed man will not grow hair by getting excited. ZAIRE

BANANAS

Little by little grow the bananas. CONGO

Lower your head modestly while passing, and you will harvest
bananas. CONGO

BARGAIN

Through lack of bargaining one loses a cheap buy. HAUSA

He who wants to barter, usually knows what is best for him. ETHIOPIA

He who wishes to barter, does not like his belongings. NIGERIA

BASKET

A basket with its bottom burst is useless. YORUBA

Do not fill your basket with useless shells of coconuts. SWAHILI

What fills the small basket doesn't fill the large one. BEMBA

A pretty basket does not prevent worries. CONGO

Even the bottom of a basket finds something to hold. MALAGASY

BAT

A bat is not a bird.   OVAMBO

BEAN

Beans are not equal to meat.   OVAMBO
One can't get beans out of wild melons.   OVAMBO
One bean spoiled the beans.   GULANI

BEARD

A long beard and a rosary will not make you a priest.   BAMBARA
A long beard does not prevent a house going to bed hungry.   FULANI

BEAST

Every beast roars in its own den.   BANTU
He doesn't kill the beast who only looks at it.   JABO
The beasts plan ahead before entering the fields.   JABO

BEAUTY

Beauty is an empty calabash.   CAMEROON
Verily, beauty is power.   KANURI
The beauty you left behind, where will you find it tomorrow?   MOROCCO
Beauty is in the oleander and the oleander is bitter.   MOROCCO
There is no beauty but the beauty of action.   MOROCCO
If you suffer in order to be beautiful, don't blame anyone but
    yourself.   GANDA
Beauty and pride go to the grave.   SWAHILI
Anyone who sees beauty and does not look at it will soon
    be poor.   YORUBA
Personal beauty does not pay a debt.   ASHANTI
If you find 'Miss This Year' beautiful, then you'll find
    'Miss Next Year' even more so.   NIGERIA
The beauty of the corn cob is apparent in the inside only.   SWAHILI
You are beautiful; but learn to work, for you cannot eat
    your beauty.   CONGO
Your beauty is in what you have.   BAGUIRMI
Beauty does no good.   KIKUYU

Bakuba cosmetic case with geometric-symbolic reliefs, Kasal region, Belgian Congo. Wood. Brussels, Coll. Baron Lambert.

Hairpin, carved in the form of superposed human figures, from the subgroup Baluba-Shankadi, Kasal region, Belgian Congo. Wood.

Beauty is not in the hair; beauty is in the cleanliness of
the skin. CAMEROON

Beauty is not in bangles, nor kindness in the skin. SOUTH AFRICA

Beautiful from behind, ugly in front. TSONGA

A beautiful thing is never perfect. EGYPT

BED

A small bed will not hold two persons. YORUBA

Stretch your legs according to the length of your bed spread. LIBYA

BEE

Better a handful of bees than a basket full of flies. MOROCCO

When the bee comes to your house, let her have beer;
you may want to visit the bee's house some day. ZAIRE

BEER

Drink beer, think beer. ZAIRE

BEETLE

However much the beetle is afraid it will not stop the lizard
swallowing it. FULANI

In his own nest a beetle is a sultan. EGYPT

Every beetle is a gazelle in the eyes of its mother. MOROCCO

BEGGAR

A beggar won't mind being insulted.

The best morsels are never given to a beggar.

Better a beggar than a thief. HAUSA

BEGINNING

If you know the beginning well, the end will not trouble you. WOLOF

Better a mistake at the beginning than at the end. CAMEROON

BETRAY

He who betrays you is not one from far away.

BELLY

The belly is not a treasurer. HAUSA

If my belly is of glass, I will fill it with bread and chicken; if it
  is a closed cellar, I will fill it with cockroaches.   TUNISIA

He who has a back is not beaten on the belly.   EGYPT

The most extensive land is the human belly.   RUANDA BURUNDI

BIGAMIST

The bigamist dies of hunger.   BUGANDA

BIG MAN

If it's a big man that is hurting you, smile at him.

You arrive Mr. Big Shot but leave Mr. Nobody.   ZULU

BIRD

A little bird for a little cage.

A bird with a beautiful plumage does not sit in the corner.

A chattering bird builds no nest.   CAMEROON

A clever bird builds its nest with other birds' feather.   SHONA

Catch soft birds with sweet words.   SOUTH AFRICA

Every little bird has a long beak.   OVAMBO

Little birds don't plunge into arrows.   OVAMBO

The little bird starts with one straw.   OVAMBO

When a big bird doesn't trouble to fly it goes to sleep
  hungry.   ASHANTI

The bird caught in the trap is the one to sing sweetly.   OJI

If the bird does not drink at the stream, it knows its own
  watering place.   WOLOF

By going and coming, a bird weaves its nest.   ASHANTI

All birds will flock to a fruitful tree.   SENEGAL

As great birds die the eggs rot.   SOUTH AFRICA

Two birds disputed about a kernel, when a third swooped
  down and carried it off.   CONGO

A bird that allows itself to be caught will find a way of
  escaping.   FULANI

When the figs are ripe all the birds want to eat.   KENYA

Do not scare the birds you are going to shoot.   MALAGASY

You may well have caught a bird, but have you a fire to
  roast it on?   MALAGASY

13

Bobo statuette of a crane, from Upper Bolta. Painted wood, ht., 21⅝ in. Brussels, private coll.

It is the softness of the lime that is fatal to the bird. MALAGASY

A big bird can't be trapped with chaff. SHONA

The bird that walks straight into the snare is bound to
be caught. HAUSA

Where there are birds, there is water. NAMIBIA

Some birds avoid the water, ducks look for it. NIGERIA

The bird can drink much, but the elephant drinks more. WOLOF

The bad bird fouls its own nest. ASHANTI

The bird flies high, but always returns to earth. NIGERIA

No bird flies and never rests. ZULU

BIRTH

Birth is the only remedy against death. HAUSA

BITTERNESS

A bitter feeling is death to the heart. ZULU

When bitterness precedes sweetness, the sweetness
becomes sweeter. ANNANG

BLACK

Black will blacken people. NYANG

Rather a black heart without words than black words
without heart. BAKONGO

BLACK MAN

The black man has a rib and a cup of blood more than the
white man. MOROCCO

BLACKSMITH

A blacksmith has no need of an axe.

No one is a blacksmith at birth. OVAMBO

BLIND

The blind say that eyes have no sense of smell. NIGERIA

If you open the eyes of a blind man he wants to go back to
the darkness. BERBER

BLOOD

Human blood is heavy; he who has shed it cannot run away.

Blood is the sweat of heroes.   RHODESIA

Blood will not wash away dirt.   NIGERIA

BLOW

One blow will not knock down the strong man.   NIGERIA

BLOW AWAY

What has been blown away, cannot be found again.   ETHIOPIA

BOAST

No one boasts of what belongs to another.   ASHANTI

He who boasts much can do little.   Niger

BOAT

A boat does not go forward if each one rows his own way.   SWAHILI

Don't buy a boat that is under water.   ZAIRE

BONE

A bone in a mortar is no luck for the dog.   HAUSA

BOOK

Reading books removes sorrows from the heart.   MOROCCO

A wise man without a book is like a workman without tools.   MOROCCO

BORROW

A borrowed fiddle does not finish a tune.   ZIMBABWE

Do not borrow from the world, for the world will require its
    own back with interest.   SWAHILI

A borrowed coat does not keep one warm.   EGYPT

BOSS

He who has a boss is not the master of his burden.   BAMBARA

BOTTLE

You can't look into a bottle with both eyes at the same time.   TOGO

BOULDER

A boulder is the father of the rocks.   YORUBA

BOW

A bow stretched to the limit will break.   ZIMBABWE

BOWL

A bowl should not laugh when a calabash breaks.

BRACELET

A single bracelet does not jingle.   CONGO

Try this bracelet: if it fits you wear it; but if it hurts you,
    throw it away no matter how much it sparkles.   KENYA

BRAGGART

A braggart is recognized by his headgear.   NAMIBIA

BRANCH

He who pulls a branch brings the leaves with it.   ILA

Don't break the branch you climbed.   OVAMBO

BREAD

A half loaf is better than no bread.   ZULU

A strawberry blossom will not moisten dry bread.   BUGANDA

However bad the bread it is better than cattle dung.   NIGERIA

The man who has bread to eat doesn't appreciate the severity
    of a famine.   YORUBA

BREAKFAST

The early breakfast is bought with gold.   MOROCCO

BRIBERY

Bribery is the enemy of justice.   SWAHILI

The man who goes to the spirit world has no bribe or ordeal. BONDEI

BRIDE

Who will speak for the bride but her mother?   EGYPT

Never argue with a new bride.   MASAI

17

A new bride should look back. ZAMBIA

We praised the bride, and she was found pregnant. TUNISIA

A young bride looks lovely, but a wife and mother looks
    lovelier. KIMBUNDU

BRIDGE

Better building bridges than building walls. SWAHILI

If you destroy a bridge, be sure you can swim. SWAHILI

BROAD

If I wanted to become broad, I would fall down in the middle of
    the road and let an elephant tread on me. HAUSA

BROTHER

Brothers love each other when they are equally rich.
A brother is like one's shoulder. SOMALIA

BUCKET

You should make a new bucket whilst you still have the
    old one. BERBER

If the bucket has been long in the well, it ought to come
    out with water. HAUSA

The well gives, but the bucket refuses. HAUSA

BUFFALO

No buffalo was ever beaten by its calf. ZULU

BULL

One cannot part two fighting bulls. WOLOF

Don't help a bull out of a ditch, for when he's out he'll
    butt you. MADAGASCAR

If the bull would throw you, lie down. NIGERIA

A bull is not known in two herds. RHODESIA

BUNDLE

Sticks in a bundle are unbreakable. KENYA

BUTCHER

The butcher has no regard for the breed of the beast. YORUBA

The butcher is not startled at the multiplicity of sheep. EGYPT

BUTTERFLY

The butterfly that flies among the thorns will tear its wings.

C

CACTUS

Cactus is bitter only to him who tastes it. ETHIOPIA

CALF

The calf is not afraid of the mother's horns.

If you see that a town worships a calf, then cut the grass
and feed it. ETHIOPIA

Do not slaughter a calf before its mother's eyes. KENYA

Calves don't follow horses. NIGERIA

CALLING

Everybody to his or her own calling and none to any other. BAKONGO

CALL OUT

Unless you call out, who will open the door? ETHIOPIA

CAMEL

The camel and his driver—each has his own plan.

The camel carries the load, but it is the tick that complains. MOROCCO

Is the white camel made of fat? BERBER

He who rides a camel should not be afraid of dogs. BERBER

One camel does not make fun of another camel's hump. GUINEA

CANOE

A canoe does not know who is king. When it turns over,
everyone gets wet. MALAGASY

A paddle here, a paddle there,—the canoe stays still. SIERRA LEONE

He who paddles two canoes, sinks.   Bemba

No man can paddle two canoes at the same time.   Bantu

A canoe is paddled on both sides.   Ivory Coast

Do not kick away the canoe which helped you to cross
    the river.   Malagasy

Carpenter

A carpenter is not a blacksmith.   Ovambo

Cat

They asked the female cat why her kittens were of different
    colors; she said she is embarrassed to say no.   Tunisia

No matter how much the world changes, cats will never
    lay eggs.   Bambara

A cat may go to a monastery, but will always remain a cat.   Ethiopia

Cat and mouse can't be neighbors long.   Ovambo

When you treat someone like a wild cat, he will steal your
    chickens.   Malagasy

If stretching were wealth, the cat would be rich.   Ghana

When the wild cat becomes a leopard, it will devour large
    beasts.   Yoruba

An old cat will never learn to dance.   Morocco

Cattle

No cattle without a dung heap.

Where the cattle are, there the wolf shall die.

Where the cattle stand together, the lion lies down hungry.

Don't mix your cattle with those of a chief.   South Africa

The cattle is as good as the pasture in which it grazes.   Ethiopia

Chameleon

Behave like the chameleon: look forward and observe
    behind.   Malagasy

Chance

Chance comes to those who know what they want.   Ashanti

One who waits for chance may wait a year.   Yoruba

CHARACTER

Character comes before the teacher. HAUSA

CHARITY

Charity doesn't come out of a prison. MOROCCO

CHEAT

A blade won't cut another blade; a cheat won't cheat
another cheat. ETHIOPIA

CHICKEN

A chicken with beautiful plumage does not sit in a corner.

A chicken that will grow into a cock can be spotted the very
day it hatches.

No chicken will fall into the fire a second time.

Even though chickens don't wash, their eggs are still
white. SIERRA LEONE

The chicken-thief does not listen to the chicken's prayer. ZANZIBAR

A chicken's head cannot wear a turban. ZANZIBAR

A chicken has no bad luck in the morning. ANNANG

The chicken also knows when it's morning, but still watches
the mouth of the cock. ASHANTI

The most stupid chicken always challenges the wildcat. BANTU

The watched chicken never lays. CONGO

In the village that you don't know, the chickens
have teeth. IVORY COAST

Do not eat your chicken and throw its feathers in the
front yard. LIBERIA

If you get mixed with bran you'll soon be pecked by chickens. LIBYA

You can't blame the axe for the noise made by the chicken
you are about to slaughter. MALAGASY

A chicken that hatches a crocodile's eggs is looking
for trouble. MALAGASY

The chicken is no match for the knife. SWAHILI

When a hen is brooding, another hen cannot sit on
her eggs. SUDAN

Every cackling hen was an egg at first. RUANDA BURUNDI

21

Pick up the hen and you can gather all the chicks. ASHANTI

Hens keep quiet when the cock is around. RUANDA BURUNDI

However full the house, the hen finds a corner to lay in. SIERRA LEONE

CHIEF

The chief is like a rubbish heap; everything comes to him. NGONE

The chief has no relative. TSONGA

Where the chief walks, there questions are decided. OVAMBO

The enemy of a chief is he who has grown up with him from
childhood. ASHANTI

Don't expect to be offered a chair when you visit a place
where the chief himself sits on the floor. GHANA

CHILDREN

The child hates the one who gives him all he wants.

If a child washes his hands he could eat with kings.

A child's fingers are not scalded by a piece of hot yam which
his mother puts into his palm.

Children are the wisdom of the nation. JABO

It takes a whole village to raise one child. YORUBA

Make a bed for the children of other people in the place
where your own children sleep. MOROCCO

Honor a child and it will honor you. ILA

It's a bad child who doesn't take advice. ASHANTI

A child that asks questions isn't stupid. EWE

The child doesn't know his father's poverty. KPELLE

A child is like a camel's neck, it goes where it pleases. MOROCCO

A child is like an axe; even if it hurts you, you still carry it
on your shoulder. BEMBA

A cranky child has not been spanked. OVAMBO

If with the right hand you flog the child, with your left hand
draw her unto your breast. YORUBA

You need not tell a child that there is a God. NZIMA

He who leaves a child lives eternally. CHAGGA

A child that has never been in a strange town thinks her
mother cooks best. HO

Hit a child and quarrel with its mother. HAUSA

Mother and child, Mayumbe region, Belgian Congo. Wood. Tervueren, Musée Royal du Congo Belge.

Mother and child, Bena Lulua style, Kasai region, Belgian Congo. Wood. Tervueren, Musée Royal du Congo Belge.

Children talk with God. BOTSWANA

A talkative child reveals his mother's secrets. KPELLE

The child who loves freedom is the first victim of it. BAMBARA

The motherless child will suckle the grandmother. BAMBARA

He who longs too much for a child will marry a pregnant
woman. BAMBARA

Don't tell any more fairy tales when the child has gone
to sleep. BURUNDI

Children of the same mother do not always agree. NIGERIA

What the child says, he has heard at home. NIGERIA

If the child robs when he begins to walk, he will plunder
a sheepfold when he grows older. WOLOF

Do not make the dress before the child is born. TANZANIA

When you show the moon to a child, it sees only your finger. ZAMBIA

Children are the reward of life. CONGO

More precious than our children are the children of our
children. EGYPT

Saying that it's for her child, she gets herself a loaf of bread. ETHIOPIA

By crawling, a child learns to stand. HAUSA

It is the duty of children to wait on elders, and not the elders
on children. KENYA

When you take a knife away from a child, give him a piece
of wood instead. KENYA

Too large a morsel chokes the child. MAURITANIA

When my child and I have eaten—then clear the table. MOROCCO

It is the woman whose child has been eaten by a witch
who best knows the evils of witchcraft. NIGERIA

When the child falls the mother weeps; when the mother
falls the child laughs. RUANDA BURUNDI

CHOOSE

Who chooses will always have desires. ZANZIBAR

CLEANSE

If you try to cleanse others—just like soap, you will waste
away in the process! MADAGASCAR

CLOTH

A white cloth and a stain never agree.   YORUBA

CLOTHES

He whose clothes are too fine, shall go about in rags.   MAURITANIA

Clothes put on while running come off while running.   ETHIOPIA

Before you ask a man for clothes, look at the clothes that
    he is wearing.   YORUBA

He who does not mend his clothes will soon have none.   NIGER

New clothes have no lice.   OVAMBO

CLOUD

Clouds do not always mean rain, but smoke is a sure sign
    of fire.

Two lightening flashes cannot come from one cloud.   BURUNDI

COBRA

The cobra knows its length.   OVAMBO

COCK

You do not need a big stick to break a cock's head.   AKAN

We do not know the cock in the egg.   ZIMBABWE

When the cock is drunk, he forgets about the hawk.   ASHANTI

COCKROACH

If the cockroach refuses to stay in its hole, the chicken
    refuses to stay hungry.   ANNANG

COCONUT

He on whose head we would break a coconut never stands still.

A coconut can't compete with a stone.   SWAHILI

He who cracks the coconut must eat the cream.   SWAHILI

Eat coconuts while you have teeth.   SENEGAL

If you had teeth of steel, you could eat iron coconuts.   SENEGAL

COLD

Cold teaches a man how to steal charcoal.   MOROCCO

If there were no cold Friday evenings and boring Saturdays,
no one would get married any more.   MOROCCO

COMPLAIN

He who complains much does little.   SWAHILI

No attention is paid to him who is always complaining.   KENYA

CONVERSATION

A good conversation is better than a good bed.   ABYSSINIA

He who begins a conversation, does not foresee the end.   MAURITANIA

COOK

When your luck deserts you, even cold food burns.   BEMBA

Do not try to cook the goat's young in the goat's milk.   BAGUIRMI

Before one cooks, one must have the meat.   MAURITANIA

If you watch your pot, your food will not burn.   MAURITANIA

Before cooking, one must have provisions.   SENEGAL

It is the pot that boils but the dish gets the credit.   CAMEROON

The food which is prepared has no master.   MALAGASY

Things that are useful to people go into the cooking pot.   ZANZIBAR

COPPER

Don't throw away your copper for the sake of gold's glitter.   SWAHILI

CORN

You can tell a ripe corn by its look.

When there is nothing to eat but corn, rice is a luxury.   HAUSA

COTTAGE

Don't praise a cottage in which you haven't yet slept.   SOUTH AFRICA

COUNTRY

Old countries don't disappear overnight; they stay for breakfast.   EGYPT

When you are looking for a country with no tombstones
you will find yourself in the land of cannibals.   MADAGASCAR

COVETOUSNESS

Covetousness is the father of unfulfilled desires.   YORUBA

27

Barotse container, Southern Rhodesia. Wood. Antwerp, Ethnografisch Museum.

Cow

A cow does not know he lost his tail till cow-fly season.   GUYANA

When mother cow is chewing grass its young ones watch
    its mouth.   IBO

A cow must graze where she is tied.   SIERRA LEONE

The cow steps on the calf, but she does not hate it.   SENEGAL

What a cow eats a calf drinks.   SENEGAL

A cow among calves doesn't grow old.   OVAMBO

A black cow also gives white milk.   SIERRA LEONE

Before you milk a cow—tie it up.   SOUTH AFRICA

However much milk the cow has it will not milk butter.   FULANI

The cow knows the cowherd but not the owner.   ETHIOPIA

A cow gave birth to a fire; she wanted to lick it, but it
    burned; she wanted to leave it, but she could not
    because it was her own child.   ETHIOPIA

I have a cow in the sky, but cannot drink her milk.   ETHIOPIA

A cow that has no tail should not try to chase away flies.   GUINEA

Coward

One who does what he says is not a coward.

In the house of the coward there is no weeping.   PEDI

Even over cold pudding, the coward says: 'It will burn
    my mouth'.   ETHIOPIA

A coward sweats in water.   ETHIOPIA

A coward is full of precaution.   SOMALIA

Cowards have no scars.   ZIMBABWE

Crab

A crab does not beget a bird.   GHANA

Crane

'What's all the fuss?' said the crane after the eel had slipped
    away. 'I never liked fish anyway.'

Crazy

Pretend that you are crazy, you will live.   TUNISIA

CREDIT

Better to sell cheap than for credit. HAUSA

CRICKET

The cricket cries, the year changes. CAMEROON

You can catch a cricket in your hand but its song is all over the field. MALAGASY

CRITICISM

I don't criticize others so that others may not criticize me. CONGO

The fetus that is afraid of criticism is never born. BURUNDI

CROCODILE

If you have escaped the jaws of the crocodile while bathing in the river, you will surely meet a leopard on the way.

The crocodile is only strong in the water. ANGOLA

A young crocodile does not cry when he falls in the water. SUDAN

Two crocodiles cannot agree. SWAHILI

The crocodile does not die under the water so that we can call the monkey to celebrate its funeral. AKAN

Only when you have crossed the river, can you say the crocodile has a lump on his snout. ASHANTI

No matter how long a log floats on the river, it will never be a crocodile. BAMBARA

The power of the crocodile is in the water. BANTU

Cross the river among a crowd and the crocodile won't eat you. MADAGASCAR

When the crocodiles leave, the caimans come. MALAGASY

A starving crocodile is never pleasant. MALAGASY

If crocodiles eat their own eggs what would they do to the flesh of a frog. NIGERIA

CRUELTY

Cruelty is the strength of the wicked.

CRY

A man who cries all the time is not heard.

CUCUMBER

The only difference between the cucumber and water is
    the moving of the teeth. TUNISIA

CURE

There is no cure that does not have its price. KENYA

CURIOSITY

Curiosity caused the roebuck to be shot in the eye. OVAMBO

There are people who place a basket on your head to see
    what you carry. WOLOF

CUSTOMS

Follow the customs or flee the country. ZULU

D

DANCE

If you can't dance well, you'd better not get up. HAUSA

If everyone is going to dance, who, then, would watch? CAMEROON

If you are dancing with your rivals, don't close your eyes. BURUNDI

When the music changes, so does the dance. HAUSA

He who is unable to dance blames it on the stony yard. KENYA

You cannot dance well on only one leg. MOZAMBIQUE

If you meet a woman on the dance floor and marry her,
    she'll someday run off with a drummer. YORUBA

DARKNESS

Darkness conceals the hippopotamus. ZULU

DAUGHTER

A silly daughter teaches her mother how to bear children. ETHIOPIA

What itches in the daughter's skirt, itches also in
    her mother's. RUANDA BURUNDI

Arched harp with carved human head. L., 25¾ in. Tervueren, Belgium, Musée Royal de l'Afrique Centrale.

Dawn

No-one knows what the dawn will bring.   ETHIOPIA

Day

Treat the days well and they will treat you well.   BEMBA
The day did not know that night had fallen.   CAMEROON
The day cuts off the promise of the night.   EGYPT

Death

The dead are not seen in the company of the living.

That which is deadly may have a sweet scent.

Death is always news.

Death is blind.   SWAHILI
What's the use of consulting a dead man's horoscope.   SENEGAL

Death is the key that will open a miser's coffers.   SIERRA LEONE

Death has no modesty.   ZULU

A person is always thanked after death.   BOTSWANA

Against the illness of death there is no medicine.   TOUCOULEURE

The priest will die; the doctor will depart his life; the
     sorcerer will not be spared.   YORUBA

Death has no heifer.   ILA

Always being in a hurry doesn't hinder death, neither does
     going slowly hinder living.   SWAHILI

Death is hiding in the corner of the blanket.   BASOTO

Death is the pursuer, the disease is the constant
     companion of people.   MADAGASCAR

Death is blind.   TSONGA

Death gives no answer.   JABO

Whatever you do you will die.   VAI

If we knew where death resided, we would never stay there. ASHANTI

Death makes no appointment.   KIKUYU

A man dies before we appreciate him.   JABO

The dying person cannot wait for the shroud to be woven. MALAGASY

Dying is cleaning, like the broom.   MADAGASCAR

When a man dies his feet get bigger.   BERBER

One is born, one dies; the land grows.   ETHIOPIA

Fear is no obstacle to death.   BAMBARA

33

A dead man does not know where his grave is. BANTU

There is no discrimination in the forest of the dead. ANNANG

Who came back from the grave and told the story? TUNISIA

DEBT

Debts make the thief. MALAGASY

DESIRE

What one desires is always better than what one has. ETHIOPIA

Desire is above gratification on the neck. KENYA

DEVIL

The devil tempts but doesn't force. GUYANA

What the devil does in a year an old woman does in an hour. MOROCCO

DEW

If you rise too early, the dew will wet you. NIGERIA

No dew ever competed with the sun. ZULU

DIARRHEA

Who suffers from diarrhea, is not not afraid of the dark. BANTU

DILIGENCE

Nothing is so difficult that diligence cannot master it. MALAGASY

DISCUSSION

Too much discussion will lead to a row. IVORY COAST

DO

He who can do nothing, does nothing. WOLOF

He who cannot do anything does nothing. GAMBIA

If you've nothing to do, dig a spinster's grave. MALI

DOCTOR

There is no doctor on the day you die. FULANI

DOG

Too many calls confuse the dog.

A dog never forgets his master.

As the dog said, 'If I fall down for you and you fall down for me, it is playing.'

A dog does not mind being called a dog.

A dog returns to where he has been fed.

Beat one dog and the others will run away.

The dog stole and the goat is being punished.	NIGERIA
A dog cannot carry its puppies on its back.	SUDAN
It is the wandering dog that finds the old bone.	SIERRA LEONE
A dog doesn't die at the hand of its master.	ZIMBABWE
If a dog bites you and you don't bite him back, it will say that you have no teeth.	SUDAN
If the tail of the dog can save me, I don't care about its stench.	TUNISIA
Do not call to a dog with a whip in your hand.	ZULU
Stroke your dog and he will steal eggs.	BANTU
The barking of the dogs will not disturb the clouds.	BERBER
A dog with a full mouth won't bark.	FULANI
When the dog isn't at home, he doesn't bark.	WOLOF
Dogs don't love people, they love the place where they are fed.	BURUNDI
If you do not step on the dog's tail, he will not bite you.	CAMEROON
The dog I bought, bit me; the fire I kindled burned me.	ETHIOPIA
A white dog does not bite another white dog.	KENYA
If you play with a dog, don't complain when it tears your clothes.	ANNANG
The dog says he will never commit adultery, but when he does so, he commits it with his own father's wife.	ASHANTI
Don't kick a sleeping dog.	MADAGASCAR
The dog's bark is not might, but fright.	MADAGASCAR
Only thin dogs become wild.	MALAGASY
Do not respond to a barking dog.	MOROCCO

DONKEY

Whoever ploughs with a team of donkeys must have patience.	ZIMBABWE
Better half a donkey than half a camel.	EGYPT

Door

Every door has its own key. SWAHILI

Dream

No one dreams of going to a place where they will kill him. IVORY COAST
Dreaming of eating won't satisfy the hungry man. FULANI

Dress

Being well dressed does not prevent one from being poor. CONGO

Droppings

Old droppings don't stink. SWAHILI

Drown

You will never drown where you always take a bath. MALI

Drum

It is very difficult to beat a drum with a sickle. HAUSA

Drunkenness

Yesterday's drunkenness will not quench today's thirst. EGYPT
Where there is drunkenness, there is trouble. SWAHILI

E

Eagle

The eagle is the prince of birds of prey. YORUBA
The flight of the eagle won't stop that of the sandfly. FULANI
The feathers of a dead eagle would cover you all over. GABON

Ear

The hollow of the ear is never full.
Ears are usually un-invited guests.
'Come and I'll tell you something,' tickles the ear.
A healthy ear can stand hearing sick words. SENEGAL

When the ear does not hear the eye will see better. GUYANA

The ears do not lose their interest. NAMIBIA

Even the sharpest ear cannot hear an ant singing. SUDAN

It's the ear that troubles the mouth. GHANA

Ancient things remain in the ears. OJI

EARTH

We have never seen the earth show her teeth.

If the earth had a mouth it would defend many. OVAMBO

Earth is the queen of beds. NIGERIA

Earth is but a marketplace; heaven is home. YORUBA

The earth is a beehive; we all enter by the same door but
live in different cells. BANTU

The earth is God's bride—she feeds the living and cherishes
the dead. MALAGASY

The earth is a giant cooking pot and men are the meat
therein. MALAGASY

Earth and heaven don't come together. GHANA

EAT

Only what you have eaten is yours; other things may not be.

People of the same blood eat from the same pot. SOTHO

Eat whatever you like, but dress as others do. EGYPT

The cultivator is one; the eaters are many. Swahili

When you have a lot to do, start with a meal. SOUTH AFRICA

The hand suffers at work, but the mouth still must eat. SUDAN

If you are looking for a fly in your food, it means that you
are full. SOUTH AFRICA

Nature gave us two cheeks to make it easier to eat hot
food. GHANA

Don't take a second mouthful before you have swallowed
the first. MADAGASCAR

You can't eat "almost". ZULU

EBB

Ebb does not follow ebb—flood is in between. SUDAN

The flood takes him in, and the ebb takes him out. CAMEROON

Eel

The eel that got away is as fat as your thigh. MADAGASCAR

Egg

The eggs teach the hen how to hatch. KWELI

If you would eat eggs, take care of the hen. NIGERIA

Eggs and iron must not be in the same bag. SUDAN

Better an egg this year than a chicken next year. ETHIOPIA

If one is not in a hurry, even an egg will start walking. ETHIOPIA

He who has an egg in his pocket does not dance. GABON

An egg in the mouth is better than a fowl in the fowlhouse. HAUSA

You cannot play with eggs on a rock slab. HAUSA

The hen lays an egg, and the cock feels the pain in his
backside. MOROCCO

Egoism

The portion that a man keeps for himself is usually not
the smallest. ZAIRE

Elephant

An elephant does not die from one broken rib.

Even if the elephant is thin he is still the lord of the jungle.

When an elephant chases you, you climb a prickly tree.

When two elephants struggle it is the grass that suffers. SWAHILI

If there were no elephants in the jungle, the buffalo would
be big. LIBERIA

Throwing pebbles at an elephant in no way disturbs him. NIGERIA

The elephant doesn't bite, it's his trunk one fears. HAUSA

You cannot kill an elephant with bullets of wax. ASHANTI

Do not waste spears on stabbing rhinos when elephants
may still show up. SHONA

The hare and the elephant don't travel well together. BAMBARA

An elephant does not get tired carrying his trunk. BURUNDI

An elephant will reach to the roof of the house. CAMEROON

A fool will pair an ox with an elephant. ETHIOPIA

However little you think of the elephant, you can't say it
won't fill a pot. FULANI

A mousetrap can not kill an elephant.   GABON

An elephant can do nothing to a tamarind tree, except to
    shake it.   WOLOF

However poor the elephant, it will be worth more than
    ten frogs.   HAUSA

The elephant's track treads out the camel's.   HAUSA

An elephant's head is no load for a child.   SIERRA LEONE

The death throes of an elephant are not so annoying as a
    living flea.   ZANZIBAR

Every elephant has to carry its own trunk around.   ZIMBABWE

Even an ant can hurt an elephant.   ZULU

It is sad when the elephant dies, but the whole tribe can feed
    on it.   SUDAN

EMBRACE

The embrace at meeting is better than at parting.   EGYPT

ENDURANCE

Endure, and drink your medicine.   KENYA

Endurance pierces marble.   MOROCCO

ENEMY

When there is no enemy within, the enemies outside cannot
    hurt you.

An intelligent enemy is better than a stupid friend.   SENEGAL

Pass by your enemy hungry but never naked.   EGYPT

Your enemy won't praise you, even though you catch a
    leopard and give it to him.   HAUSA

Better an enemy of the wise than a friend of the fool.   EGYPT

ENOUGH

Where there is more than enough, more than enough is
    wasted.   BANTU

ENVY

Envy is prosperity's manure.   FULANI

From the well of envy, only a fool drinks the water.   HAUSA

39

ETERNITY

Eternity gives no answer.

LIBERA

EUROPE

If there had been no poverty in Europe, then the white man would have come to spread his clothes in Africa.

OJI

EVENING

You must decide where you are going in the evening, if you intend to leave early in the morning.

MALI

EVENT

Events follow one another like the days of the week.

TANZANIA

EVIL

Evil enters like a needle and spreads like an oak tree.

ETHIOPIA

Evil knows where evil sleeps.

NIGERIA

It is more fun doing evil than putting it right.

NIGERIA

He who sows evil will harvest repentance.

MOROCCO

Evil deeds are like perfume; difficult to hide.

JABO

He who does evil, expects evil.

GUINEA

EVIL MAN

An evil man is like a stump in the road—if you stumble over him, you either fall down or injure yourself.

GHANA

EXECUTIONER

The executioner never lets the sword be passed across his own neck.

YORUBA

EXILE

Exile is the brother of death.

BERBER

EXPENSES

Proportion your expenses to what you have, not what you expect.

HAUSA

EXPERT

Two experts never agree.

ZIMBABWE

Eye

The eye envies, not the ear.

The eye never forgets what the heart has seen. BANTU

The eye is a thief. EFIK

The eye cannot see what blows into it. TUAREG

Let him speak who has seen with his eyes. CONGO

No better witnesses than your own eyes. ETHIOPIA

To have two eyes can be cause for pride; but to have one
eye is better than to have none. GUINEA

Eyes do not eat but know what will satisfy. FULANI

When the eyes don't see, the heart doesn't grieve. EGYPT

Never give up what you have seen for what you have heard. SWAHILI

F

Face

A beautiful face doesn't need adornment. SWAHILI

A shining face goes with a full belly. HAUSA

Fall

Do not laugh at the fallen; you may find slippery roads ahead.

If you don't stand for something, you will fall for something.

Even the fall of a dancer is a somersault. SENEGAL

However hard a thing is thrown into the air, it always falls to
the ground. HAUSA

Everything above falls to earth at the end. HAUSA

Don't look where you fell, but where you slipped. LIBERIA

One man's fall is another's uprising. FULANI

Falsehood

When falsehood goes around it goes astray. EGYPT

False Step

In every false step there is something good. MOROCCO

FAMILIARITY

Familiarity breeds contempt; distance breeds respect. NIGER

If familiarity were useful water wouldn't cook fish. FULANI

Familiarity is like the sea that kills the fisherman. UGANDA

FAMILY

The family is like the forest, if you are outside it is dense, if
you are inside you see that each tree has its own position. AKAN

Dine with a stranger but save your love for your family. ETHIOPIA

FAMINE

Famine compels one to eat the fruit of all kinds of trees. YORUBA

FAMOUS

He who wants to be famous will have many a sleepless night. TUNISIA

FARM

He who neglects his farm will not see a bright eye in his house. HAUSA

FATE

Let no man think he can escape his fate.

FATHER

If you know his father and grandfather, don't worry about his son.

When you follow in the path of your father, you learn to walk
like him. ASHANTI

No one will say 'My father is incontinent'. Everyone will say
'He is a man of advice and wisdom'. TUNISIA

One father can feed seven children, but seven children
cannot feed one father. CAMEROON

I could tell better where my father's shadow groans tonight.
I could tell better where he groans. ZAIRE

FAULT

A fault confessed is half redressed. ZULU

He who is free of faults, will never die. ZAIRE

If your pocket gets empty, your faults will be many. LIBYA

Pear-shaped container with incised geometric patterns, Mayumbe region, Belgian Congo. Wood. Tervueren, Musée Royal du Congo Belge.

Fear

Fear has laughter in it; fierceness has mournings. NYANG

Fear in the forest is shame at home. HAUSA

If you fear something, you give it power over you. MOROCCO

Too much fear creates slavery. SWAHILI

Feather

The feathers make the fowl big. ASHANTI

Fence

No fence is built for the eyes. OVAMBO

Fever

He who has a fever is not shown to the fire. BEMBA

Fig

The most beautiful fig may contain a worm. ZULU

He ate one fig and he thought the autumn had come. TUNISIA

Fight

If the fight is tomorrow, why then clench your fist today? CAMEROON

Don't join in a fight if you don't have weapons. SWAHILI

If we don't fight we remain equals, if we do fight then one
of us wins. MALAGASY

Find

Soon found soon lost. KENYA

Finger

One finger alone cannot even kill a louse. KENYA

One finger can't catch a mother louse. NYANG

No one puts his finger back where it was once bitten. KIKUYU

Fingers which catch dirty fingers can be washed. BEMBA

It is best to bind up the finger before it is cut. BASUTOLAND

A handsome finger get a ring put round it. SWAHILI

44

FIRE

Fire does not make fire, only ashes.

A distant fire does not burn.   SWAHILI

Fire and gunpowder are not bedfellows.   ASHANTI

Fire purges everything.   BERBER

The fire cannot be put out with your hands.   CAMEROON

Fire has no brother.   NIGERIA

The fire that burns a royal palace only enhances its splendour.   NIGERIA

Each end of the fire has its smoke.   HAUSA

It's a low fire that warms the soup.   SHONA

Only he who treads on the fire feels it.   LIBYA

The only insurance against fire is to have two houses.   HAUSA

FISH

The fishes envy the carp on account of his shears.

A rotten fish pollutes the whole kitchen.   SENEGAL

A big fish is caught with big bait.   SIERRA LEONE

The fish caught in the net starts to think.   ZANZIBAR

He who digs too deep for a fish, may come out with a snake.   ETHIOPIA

If you find no fish, you have to eat bread.   GHANA

Fishing without a net is just bathing.   HAUSA

Once a fish is mature, it ventures into the deep.   ANNANG

Fish eat fish and he who has no might dies.   LIBYA

From all the fish in the pot you can only make one soup.   MALAGASY

FLATTER

The flatterer walks in the middle of the road.   OVAMBO

He who flatters with laughter wants to see you cry.   MOROCCO

FLAVOR

Two flavors confuse the palate.   IVORY COAST

FLEA

You can only know the fleas in the bed you have slept in.

A flea can trouble a lion more than the lion can harm a flea.   KENYA

Flint

Flint and gunpowder: every time they meet there is an explosion.   MALAGASY

Flower

For the benefit of the flowers, we water the thorns, too.   EGYPT

An old flower and a fresh flower both have good features.   DAMA

Fly

The flight of the eagle will not stop that of the sand fly.

The biting fly gets nothing by alighting on the back of the tortoise.   ASHANTI

The biting fly has no one to come to his aid in trouble.   ASHANTI

The fly heeds not death; eating is all to him.   YORUBA

A fly is nothing; yet it creates loathsomeness.   EGYPT

When a fly does not get up off a dead body, he is buried with it.   ASHANTI

A fly does not mind dying in coconut cream.   SWAHILI

The fly has no pity for the thin man.   CONGO

A fly will not get into a closed mouth.   MOROCCO

He acts like a dog who drives the flies away from food it has spurned.   LIBERIA

Even flies have ears.   TANZANIA

Fondle

What I fondle and nurse belongs to me.   MAORI

Food

Food you will not eat you do not boil.

Even the best cooking pot will not produce food.

Better that you should be made to wait for food than that food should be made to wait for you.   HAUSA

Fool

Only a fool tests the depth of the water with both feet.

A fool laughs at himself.   OVAMBO

A fool is a wise man's ladder.   SOUTH AFRICA

The fool who owns an ox is seldom recognised as a fool.   SOUTH AFRICA

We start as fools and become wise through experience.   TANZANIA

Only a fool tries to jump in the fire.   UGANDA

A fool is a treasure to the wise.   BOTSWANA

When the fool does not succeed in bleaching ebony he tries to blacken ivory.   AMHARIC

Foolishness often precedes wisdom.   BAKONGO

There is medicine for madness, but not for foolishness.   SWAHILI

By the time the fool has learned the game, the players have dispersed.   ASHANTI

It's the fool's sheep that breaks loose twice.   ASHANTI

The fool is thirsty in the midst of water.   ETHIOPIA

A fool looks for dung where the cow never grazed.   ETHIOPIA

The fool speaks, the wise man listens.   ETHIOPIA

A fool and water will go the way they are directed.   ETHIOPIA

When a fool is cursed, he thinks he is being praised.   ETHIOPIA

He who claps his hands for the fool to dance is no better than the fool.   YORUBA

Everybody loves a fool, but nobody wants him for a son.   IVORY COAST

FOOLISH DEED

A foolish deed done over again will not improve things.

After a foolish deed comes remorse.   KENYA

FOOT

The foot doesn't stay where there's no ground.   HAUSA

The man on his feet carries off the share of the man sitting down.   GUINEA

The feet rest but the heart is not at ease.   FULANI

The foot that travels the road is the one that is pricked by the thorn.   JABO

I only have my nails to scratch with and my feet to walk on.   BERBER

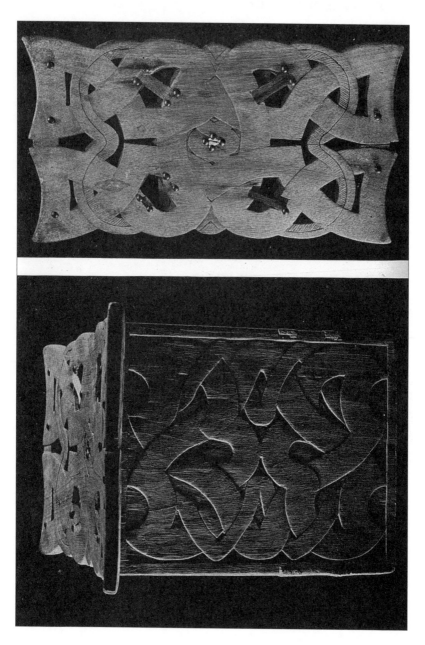

Art of Bush Negroes. Two details of a wooden stool, view from side and from above. Evanston, Ill., M. J. and F. S. Herskovits Coll.

FOOTFALL

Visitor's footfalls are like medicine; they heal the sick.   BANTU

FOOTPRINT

Nobody buys the footprint of a bullock.   OJI

FOREST

Do not call the forest that shelters you a jungle.   ASHANTI

To one who knows no better, a small garden is a forest.   ETHIOPIA

When building a house, don't measure the timbers in
the forest.   LIBERIA

A forest would want to be burned by its own wood.   MOORISH

FORGIVE

He that forgives gains the victory.   YORUBA

If there were no wrongdoing, there would be no forgiveness.   EGYPT

If you offend, ask for pardon; if offended, forgive.   ETHIOPIA

FORTUNE-TELLER

'If it is not a boy it will be a girl,' says the fortune-teller.   MALAGASY

FOWL

The disobedient fowl obeys in a pot of soup.   BENIN

The fowl digs out the blade that kills it.   SOMALIA

Fowls will not spare a cockroach that falls in their mist.   AKAN

Save your fowl before it stops flapping.   IVORY COAST

When you cook a guinea fowl, the partridge gets a
headache.   NIGERIA

In a court of fowls, the cockroach never wins his case.   RUANDA BURUNDI

No one makes a fowl taboo and then eats his chickens.   ASHANTI

FRIENDSHIP

There are three friends in this world: courage, sense, and insight.

A wound inflicted by a friend does not heal.

The more intimate the friendship the deadlier the enmity.

A friend is worth more than a brother.   CAMEROON

Friendship that is kept up only while eyes see eyes, does not go to the heart. YORUBA

Friendship slays many evils. GANDA

True friendship outlives relationship. BANTU

Friendship does not need pepper to cry. CONGO

No friendship, except after enmity. EGYPT

Even a little thing brings friendship to remembrance. GANDA

To give to thy friend is not to cast away, it is to store for the future. SWAHILI

Better a clever friend than a blundering friend. SWAHILI

Anger with our friend, rather than constant friendship with our enemy. EGYPT

Hold on to a true friend with both hands. NIGERIA
Friendship is honey—but don't eat it all. MOROCCO

A friend will wipe away sweat but not blood. IVORY COAST

An onion shared with a friend tastes like roast lamb. EGYPT

To be without a friend is to be poor indeed. SOMALIA

If your friend is honey, don't lick him thoroughly. TUNISIA

Your friend chooses pebbles for you and your enemy counts your faults. EGYPT

Friendship doubles joy and halves grief. EGYPT

A small house can lodge a hundred friends. EGYPT

An eye and a friend are quickly hurt. ETHIOPIA

A close friend can become a close enemy. ETHIOPIA

A powerful friend becomes a powerful enemy. ETHIOPIA

If a friend hurts you, run to your wife. ETHIOPIA

Bad friends prevent you from having good friends. GABON

You may laugh at a friend's roof; don't laugh at his sleeping accommodation. KENYA

Friendship reminds us of fathers, love of mothers. MALAGASY

May your friendship not be like a stone: if it breaks you cannot put the pieces together. May it be like iron: when it breaks, you can weld the pieces back together. MALAGASY

Better to lose a little money than a little friendship. MALAGASY

A stone from the hand of a friend is an apple. MAURITANIA

Only equals can be friends.	ETHIOPIA
When you know who his friend is, you know who he is.	SENEGAL
An intelligent foe is better than a stupid friend.	PEUL

FRIENDLY

A friendly person is never a good-for-nothing.	NIGERIA
Greet everyone cordially when you don't know who your in-laws are going to be.	MADAGASCAR

FRIGHT

Fright is worse than a blow.	MOROCCO

FROG

If you see a frog squatting in his house, don't ask him for a chair.	TOGO
When the master is away, the frogs hop in.	BUGANDA
When the ducks are quacking the frogs take it as a warning.	MALAGASY
The frog does not jump in the daytime without reason.	NIGERIA

FRUIT

The fruit must have a stem before it grows.	JABO

FUEL

The fuel in the lamp consumes itself but lights others.

FUR

Those with the same fur enter the same hole.	FULANI

G

GADFLY

Only a gadfly can sit on an elephant's back.   HAUSA

GAIT

Nobody walks with another man's gait.   KENYA

GAMBLER

Helping a gambler is like throwing a hair into the fire.   MOROCCO

GARDEN

A garden without a fence is like a dog without a tail.   MOROCCO

GARMENT

Whoever has only one garment does not wash it when it rains.

GIANT

It is not only giants that do great things.   JABO

GIFT

He who refuses a gift will not fill his barn.   SIERRA LEONE

Mutual gifts cement friendship.   IVORY COAST

If you receive a gift don't measure it.   KENYA

One does not give a gift without a motive.   MALI

What you give you get, ten times over.   YORUBA

What you give to others bears fruit for yourself.   SENEGAL

GIRL

Away from home the girl picks forbidden fruit.   BANTU

A young girl who is used to young men always goes
    downwards.   ETHIOPIA

A long gram of straw brings birds to the field—beautiful
    girls bring young boys to the house.   OVAMBO

If you love the girl you have to love her mother too.   ZAIRE

52

A girl may reject you and go to someone else, but no girl
ever married a wild animal.   ZULU

The tree is full of fruit, do not think it is so fertile by itself;
they have ploughed around it.

Do not think a girl has grown up to be beautiful purely and
simply. Her parents have brought her up.   TSONGA

GLUTTON

A glutton is never satisfied.   NAMIBIA

GNU (WILDEBEEST)

The wildebeest is not touched.   ZULU

GOAT

Goats cannot live in a herd of leopards.

One bad goat will spoil the herd.

Beware of the goat that is in the lion's lair.   BAMBARA

Just because he harmed your goat, do not go out and kill
his bull.   KENYA

One goat cannot carry another goat's tail.   NIGERIA

Dead goats don't fear knives.   GA

GOD

He who does not know is forgiven by God.

He who gives to God does not go to bed hungry.

The plant God favors will grow even without rain.

God made the sea, we make the ship; He made the wind,
we make the sail; He made the calm, we make oars.   SWAHILI

We decide our affairs, then we rest them with God.   JABO

To commit ten sins against God is better than to commit
one sin against a servant of God.   MOROCCO

God gives and does not remind us continually of it; the
world gives and constantly reminds us.   NUPE

Every knot has an unraveller in God.   EGYPT

God provides even for the insect between two stones.   EGYPT

If you are going to ask from God, take a big receptacle.   HAUSA

A riddle made by God has no solution.   BEMBA

Do not blame God for having created the tiger, but thank Him for not giving it wings. ABYSSINIA

God gives nothing to those who keep their arms crossed. BAMBARA

Do not walk in God's ways on someone else's behalf. BAMBARA

If God were not forgiving, heaven would be empty. BERBER

God pardons the ignorant. BERBER

God gives, but he doesn't sell. BURUNDI

God speaks a foreign tongue. OVAMBO

The opportunity that God sends does not wake up him who is asleep. SENEGAL

Where God cooks, there is no smoke. ZAMBIA

Leave the battle to God and rest your head upon your hand. YORUBA

To deny God's existence is like jumping with your eyes closed. MALAGASY

Better to be guilty in the eyes of men than in the eyes of God. MALAGASY

It is impossible to bend the arm of God. MASAI

Manage with bread and salted butter until God brings something to eat with it. MOROCCO

When one is in trouble, one remembers God. NIGERIA

Good

That which is exceptionally good is a forerunner of something bad.

Good things sell themselves; those that are bad have to be advertised.

Anticipate the good so that you may enjoy it. ETHIOPIA

A good action is better than a bad action. WOLOF

A good deed is something one returns. GUINEA

Perform good deeds; you will not regret them. MOROCCO

To bring good luck is better than to be handsome. GHANA

A good name is more valuable than a velvet garment. MOROCCO

Gossip

Gossips always suspect that others are talking about them. YORUBA

Cursing follows gossip. SHONA

Gossiping and lying are brother and sister. KENYA

He who chatters with you will chatter about you. EGYPT

54

Gourd

Until the last gourd has been broken, let us not talk of
drought.   Yoruba

Government

An unjust government is better than corrupt subjects.   Morocco

Granary

Build a granary with new posts and the rats will come looking;
build a granary with old posts and the rats will leave it alone.

Grasshopper

One can't give a grasshopper to a child if one has not
caught it yet.   Malagasy

Grateful

If something that was going to chop off your head only
knocked off your cap, you should be grateful.   Yoruba

Gratitude

Gratitude is a lotus flower whose leaves soon wither.

Great Affair

A great affair covers up a small matter.   Yoruba

Great Man

Great men have big hearts.   Ethiopia

Greatness

Greatness is not achieved with violence.

You are not great just because you say you are. South Africa

Grown-up

A grown-up who follows children is a fool.   Ghana

Grumbler

The grumbler does not leave his job, but he discourages
possible applicants.   Ganda

Guest

A guest who breaks the dishes of his host is not soon
    forgotten.

Treat your guest as a guest for two days—then on the third
    day give him a hoe.

A person is a guest for one or two days, but becomes an
    intruder on the third.   HAUSA

Do not leave your host's house, throwing mud in his well.   ZULU

We let him in, and now he shows us the door.   BERBER

Invite people into your parlour, and they will come into
    your bedroom.   SIERRA LEONE

They ate our food, and forgot our names.   TUNISIA

Guile

Guile excels strength.   FULFULDE

Guilty

Guilt is like the footprint of a hippopotamus.   NIGERIA

He who is guilty has much to say.   ASHANTI

The whip hits at the legs, not the guilt.   NIGERIA

Gun

If you have run out of gunpowder, use your gun as a club.   NIGERIA

Pipe bowl. Ht., 3⅛ in. Tervueren, Belgium, Musée Royal de l'Afrique Centrale.

Bush Negro combs. Wood. Evanston, Ill., M. J. and F. S. Herskovits Coll.

H

HAIR

Before one has white hairs, one must first have them black. SENEGAL

Even in the freshest of milk, you will still find hairs. BAMBARA

HAND

Practice with the left hand while the right is still there.

One hand can't tie a bundle. BASA

The palm of your hand will not obscure the sun. TUAREG

The attacks of the wild beast cannot be averted with only
bare hands. SOUTH AFRICA

Empty hands only please their owner. UGANDA

Without fingers the hand would be a spoon. WOLOF

Be like the mouth and the hand: when the hand is hurt the
mouth blows on it, when the mouth is hurt the hand
rubs it. MALAGASY

HANDSOME

A handsome man will not be sought after, but even a plain
girl will be run after eagerly. MAORI

HARE

If the hare is your enemy, admit that he can run fast. BAMBARA

HASTE

Haste bequeaths disappointment.

Haste has no blessing. SWAHILI

HATE

He who hates, hates himself. ZULU

When you hate someone then you seduce his wife. ASHANTI

There is no medicine to cure hatred. ASHANTI

HAWK

The hawk does not swoop on a stone unless there is a piece
of meat on it. HAUSA

59

HEAD

Where there is a head, one doesn't put the headdress on
the knee.
    Ho

HEAL

Before healing others, heal yourself.
    GAMBIA

HEART

The house of the heart is never full.

A proud heart can survive a general failure because such a
failure does not prick its pride.

When the heart acts the body is its slave.

The heart is like deep waters.
    TSONGA

The heart cannot hold two.
    EGYPT

The heart is a marketplace.
    GANDA

Keep your tents apart and your hearts together.
    TUAREG

Hearts become tired and should have recreation.
    EGYPT

That which is loved by the heart is the remedy.
    KENYA

Wear out, body! Remain, o heart.
    NBDELE

A melancholic look is visible but not a melancholic heart.
    ETHIOPIA

It is the heart which carries one to Hell or to Heaven.
    KANURI

The ailment of the heart is known to only one.
    ZULU

The bitter heart eats its owner.
    BANTU

The heart is not a knee that can be bent.
    SENEGAL

The heart is a like a goat that has to be tied up.
    SOUTH AFRICA

A letter from the heart can be read on the face.
    SWAHILI

There is no blindness but the blindness of the heart.
    TUNISIA

Rather a piece of bread with a happy heart than wealth
with grief.
    EGYPT

Whoever lets himself be led by the heart will never lose
his way.
    EGYPT

If the heart is sad, tears will flow.
    ETHIOPIA

Hearts do not meet one another like roads.
    KENYA

HEAVEN

Heaven and Earth shall never meet.

Only heaven can see the back of a sparrow.
    BANTU

HELL

In hell there are no fans.

HELP

The more help in the cornfield the smaller the harvest.   ZIMBABWE

HERE AND NOW

If it's not here and now, who cares about what and when?

HERITAGE

Only a fool points to his heritage with his left hand.   GHANA

HIDE

Don't cough in a hiding place.   SUDAN
You can burn down a house, but can you hide the smoke?   BUGANDA
There is no cure for him who hides an illness.   ETHIOPIA
You cannot hide behind your finger.   GHANA
If you are in hiding, don't light a fire.   ASHANTI

HILL

He who inherits a hill must climb it.   MOORISH
If the hill is on fire the grasshoppers are roasted.   MALAGASY
No hill without gravestones, no valley without shadows.   SOUTH AFRICA
When the rain falls in the valley, the hill gets angry.   YORUBA

HIPPOPOTAMUS

The hippopotamus that shows itself doesn't upset the boat.

HOLY MAN

Follow the holy man no farther than his threshold.   EGYPT

HOME

Not the place where I was born but where I hang my hat
    is home.
Where I make a living, there is my home.   SOMALIA
The ruin of a nation begins in the homes of its people.   ASHANTI
Living is worthless for one without a home.   ETHIOPIA
A home without a woman is like a barn without cattle.   ETHIOPIA

61

Affairs of the home should not be discussed in the
public square.   KENYA

HONEY

Once a baboon has tasted honey it does not touch
earth again.   TSONGA

He who requires honey should be patient of the
stinging bees.   MOROCCO

HOPE

Hope is the pillar of the world.   KANURI

Hope does not disappoint.   XHOSA

He who hopes fares better than he who wishes, and he who
wishes fares better than he who despairs.   MOROCCO

HORIZON

The horizon will not disappear as you run towards it. BANTU

HORNS

Horns are not too heavy for the cow.   ETHIOPIA

Horns do not grow before the head.   NIGERIA

HORSE

The horse never refuses a homeward gallop.

A horse has four legs, yet it often falls.   ZULU

Don't trust the horses if they run away, or the whores if
they repent.   TUNISIA

The horse that arrives early gets good drinking water. ZULU

When he looked under the saddle he lost his horse.   ETHIOPIA

Don't look for speed in a cheap horse; be content if it neighs. HAUSA

If you see him riding on a bamboo-cane, say to him, 'Good
health to your horse!'   MOROCCO

HOSPITALITY

Abuse of hospitality breaks the bridge.   BEMBA

HOUSE

The house roof fights the rain, but he who is sheltered
ignores it.   NIGERIA

A house with two keys is worth nothing. CONGO

No matter how many chores you finish in your house,
there is always more to be done. BAMBARA

You cannot build a house for last year's summer. ETHIOPIA

Mud houses don't burn. HAUSA

It is not the fire in the fireplace which warms the house,
but the couple who get along well. MALAGASY

If you are building a house and a nail breaks, do you
stop building, or do you change the nail? RUANDA BURUNDI

Every man who wishes to master his house must first
master his emotions. EGYPT

HOUSEWIFE

The wood brought home by the housewife can be made
into a whip to beat her with. CHAD

HUMBLE

The humble pay for the mistakes of their betters. BAGUIRMI

HUNGER

Hunger is felt by slave and king alike. ASHANTI

Today's hunger does not share itself with tomorrow's
hunger. BAMBARA

He who has eaten doesn't make a fire for the hungry. BASA

You learn a lot about a man by his behavior when hungry. ZAMBIA

He is truly hungry who accepts defeat in a fight over
meat. MADAGASCAR

Only the man who is not hungry says the coconut has a
hard shell. ABYSSINIA

When a woman is hungry, she says, 'Roast something for
the children that they may eat.' ASHANTI

What reveals a man is his behaviour in time of hunger. BEMBA

The tree knot spoils the branches; hunger spoils love. NIGERIA

When hunger gets inside you, nothing else can. YORUBA

Plenty sits still, hunger is a wanderer. ZULU

One day of hunger is not starvation. CONGO

He who does not cultivate his field, will die of hunger. GUINEA

Female figure with Baluba (Belgian Congo) characteristics, found in Northern Rhodesia. Wood. London, British Museum.

HUNT

Noise and hunting don't go together.

Hunt in every jungle, for there is wisdom and good hunting in all of them.

He who hunts two rats, catches none. BUGANDA

The hunter who always comes home with meat is a thief. BANTU

To kill only one iguana is a shame for the hunter; but a man who marries four wives is praised in the land. MOZAMBIQUE

If the hunter comes back with mushrooms, don't ask him how his hunt was. ASHANTI

The hunter does not rub himself in oil and lie by the fire to sleep. NIGERIA

The hunter in pursuit of an elephant does not stop to throw stones at birds. UGANDA

Slowly, slowly one must stalk the monkey through the bush. WOLOF

HURT

Whoever wants to hurt never misses his target. BERBER

HUSBAND

Seven children won't hold a husband, but plenty of wisdom will. MADAGASCAR

A woman's clothes are the price her husband pays for peace. BANTU

A woman cannot be proud of her husband unless he gives her children. KAONDE

A woman gets her beauty from her husband. ASHANTI

The husband's death is the widow's sorrow. YORUBA

The wise husband lives in peace with four wives. SWAHILI

Without a husband you are naked. OVAMBO

HYENA

When the hyena is gone, the dog begins to bark. ETHIOPIA

Never let a hyena know how well you can bite. KENYA

The hyena chasing two antelopes at the same time will go to bed hungry. MALI

Hyenas are caught with stinking bait. NIGERIA

A careful hyena lives a long time. RHODESIA

HYPOCRISY

Hypocrisy is the mother of peace. Moorish

IDLENESS

Idleness moves so slowly that it will be overtaken
by misery. MALAGASY

IDOL

No matter how well an idol is made, it must have
something to stand on.

IGNORANCE

There are three things that if a man does not know, he
cannot live long in this world: what is too much for him,
what is too little for him and what is just right for him. SWAHILI

Every smart man is an ignoramus that abuses his
ignorance. CAMEROON

IMPOTENT

The impotent man does not eat spicy foods. ZAIRE

INDECISION

Indecision is like the stepchild: if he doesn't wash his
hands, he is called dirty; if he does, he is wasting
the water. MADAGASCAR

INDOLENT

The indolent person reckons religious fasting a labor. YORUBA

INFLATED

What is inflated too much, will burst into fragments.   ETHIOPIA

INGRATITUDE

Ingratitude is sooner or later fatal to its author.   IVORY COAST

Do not tell the man who is carrying you that he stinks.   SIERRA LEONE

People don't count what they get—they count what they
    don't get.   KENYA

INHERIT

You inherit from the dead—not from the sick.   ZAIRE

Those who inherit fortunes are frequently more of a
    problem than those who made them.   ZAIRE

An heir also inherits quarrels.   NAMIBIA

INJUSTICE

Equality in injustice is justice.   EGYPT

It is better to be the victim of injustice than to be unjust
    yourself.   CAMEROON

INTELLIGENCE

He who has no intelligence is happy with it.   SOUTH AFRICA

INTENTION

If your intention is pure you can walk on the sea.   SWAHILI

IRON

The iron never takes advice from the hammer.   CONGO

Iron does not clang by itself.   MALAGASY

ITCH

An itching palm is a sign of good luck.   LE SOTHO

IVORY

When wood breaks, it can be repaired.
    But ivory breaks forever. . . .   YORUBA

J

JAVELIN

A javelin without blood is not a javelin.   ETHIOPIA

JEALOUSY

Jealousy starts from the eyes.   ZULU

Jealousy was boiled in the same pot as a stone; the stone
    got soft and jealousy remained.   DUALA

It is better to be the object of jealousy, than of pity.   MOROCCO

Jealousy can change a man into a leopard.   ZAIRE

A quarrel born of jealousy does not end in a hurry.   YORUBA

JOURNEY

The journey of folly has to be travelled a second time.   BONDEI

No one can leave his character behind him when he goes
    on a journey.   YORUBA

Choose your fellow traveller before you start on your journey.   HAUSA

JOY

The body of Joy is not so big.   NIGERIA

JUDAS

Even if Christ's death could have been prevented, Judas
    would still be a traitor.   ETHIOPIA

JUDGE

If the judge is against you you should withdraw the
    complaint.   MOROCCO

JUNGLE

The jungle is stronger than the elephant.   PEUL

JUSTICE

Justice becomes injustice when it makes two wounds on a
    head which only deserves one.   BAKONGO

K

KEY

The key that opens is also the key that locks.

KINDNESS

Kindness can pluck the hairs of a lion's mustache. SUDAN

A well educated man always has a kind word to say about
    the place where he spends the night. BERBER

KING

Looking at a king's mouth one would never think he sucked
    his mother's breast.

A big chair does not make a king. SUDAN

The multitude is stronger than the king. TUNISIA

When a king has good counsellors, his reign is peaceful. ASHANTI

Being happy is better than being king. HAUSA

The king inherits a country—the people only hard work. MALAGASY

When the king reigns it is thanks to the people; when a
    river sings it's thanks to the stones. MALAGASY

The king's ambassador is without sin. NIGERIA

The bone given to you by the king is meat. OVAMBO

Kings have no friends. PEUL

KITCHEN

The kitchen is older than the mosque. BAMBARA

KNIFE

The knife that has been lent, never comes back alone.

A knife does not know who is its master. ASHANTI

One knife will not cut another knife; one cheat will not
    cheat another cheat. ZAIRE

If your mouth were a knife, it would cut off your lips. ZIMBABWE

Knot

There is bound to be a knot in a very long string. GHANA

Knowledge

No one is without knowledge except he who asks no questions.

Knowledge is like a garden: if it is not cultivated, it cannot be
harvested. GUINEA

Knowledge is better than riches. CAMEROON

Not to know is bad; not to want to know is worse. WOLOF

What you don't know, you will not recognise. CAMEROON

Who does not know one thing knows another. KENYA

Nobody tells all he knows. SENEGAL

There are three things which if one does not know, one
cannot live long in the world: what is too much for one,
what is too little for one, and what is just right for one. SWAHILI

L

Laugh

If someone makes you laugh it is not always because he
loves you. KIKUYU

Laughter

Laughter gives confidence; its absence causes dispute. TAMASHEK

Law

To love the law is to lose money. MADAGASCAR

Lazy

The lazy one is pregnant in the sowing season. BURUNDI

To try and fail is not laziness. SIERRA LEONE

Leak

That which leaks cannot stay full. OVAMBO

LEARN

He who learns, teaches.   ETHIOPIA

LENDING

Lending is the firstborn of poverty.   NIGERIA

LEOPARD

Try not to get hold of a leopard's tail, but if you do—don't
    let go.   ETHIOPIA

When the leopard is away, his cubs are eaten.   RUANDA BURUNDI

LETTER

A letter from the heart can be read on the face.   SWAHILI

LIAR

The path of a liar is short.   SWAHILI

If you are a liar, recollect.   EGYPT

Believe the liar up to the door of his house and no further
    than that.   EGYPT

LIE

A lie has many variations, the truth none.

The burden of a lie is like a large tin of coals burning
    fiercely on the head of its carrier.   MOZAMBIQUE

One lie can fill a sack; a second will empty it again.   MOORISH

He who tells no lies will not grow up.   UGANDA

A smooth lie is better than a coarse truth.   EGYPT

Except for my father and my mother everybody lies.   BERBER

When the master of the house tells a lie, then offer him
    a chair.   BURUNDI

One lie ruins a thousand truths.   GHANA

The end of an ox is beef, and the end of a lie is grief.   MADAGASCAR

LIFE

Life is a shadow and a mist; it passes quickly by, and is
    no more.   MADAGASCAR

Without life there is nothing.   ZULU

Life's caravan never turns back. SWAHILI

Life is like a ballet performance—danced only once. MALI

Living is not a reward and dying is no crime. MALAGASY

LION

The lion which kills is not the one that roars. XHOSA

A brave man is scared of a lion three times; first when
  he sees the tracks; second when he hears the first roar
  and third when they are face to face. SOMALIA

It's easy to say 'May Allah roast the lion's mother', when
  the lion isn't there. MOORISH

Once a man has been bitten by a lion, he buys a dog. MOZAMBIQUE

Even a weak lion is not bitten by a dog. NAMIBIA

As long as you stay in a group, the lion will stay hungry. NIGERIA

The lion's power lies in our fear of him. NIGERIA

Until the lions have their historians, tales of the hunt shall
  always glorify the hunter. NIGERIA

A roaring lion kills no game. RHODESIA

Who is brave enough to tell the lion that his breath smells? BERBER

What is said over the dead lion's body, could not be said
  to him alive. CONGO

When spiders' webs unite, they can tie up a lion. ETHIOPIA

LISTEN

Always listen. Be careful when you speak because the bush
  has ears. GUYANA

LITTLE

Better little than too little. CAMEROON

LIZARD

The smaller the lizard the greater the hope of becoming
  a crocodile.

The lizard that jumped from the high iroko tree to the ground
  said he would praise himself if no one else did.

LOAD

What is really a load should not be called an ornament.

LOCUST

Don't try to get blood from a locust; God didn't put it in there.

LOBSTER

A lobster loves water, but not when he's being cooked in it.   SENEGAL

LOOK

A stern look is not a slap on the face.

The very fact that we are looking for something usually stands
    in the way of our finding it.

LOUSE

As long as there are lice in the seams of the garment there
    must be bloodstains on the fingernails.   YORUBA

LOVE

There is no physician who can cure the disease of love.
Love paralyzes the joints.   BOTSWANA

Love is an illness and the loved one is the only medicine.   SWAHILI

If love is a sickness, patience is the remedy.   FULANI

Love has no disputings.   KENYA

To love someone who does not love you, is like shaking a
    tree to make the dew drops fall.   CONGO

Love is like a seed; it does not choose the ground on which
    it falls.   ZULU

Love is like young rice: transplanted, still it grows.   MADAGASCAR

Love is like a baby: it needs to be treated tenderly.   ZAIRE

Love is like seaweed, even if you have pushed it away,
    that will not prevent it coming back.   CAMEROON

Love has to be shown by deeds not words.   SWAHILI

Love takes his wife to attend a meeting.   IBO

Love is better than a whip.   NIGERIA

One thread for the needle, one love for the heart.   SUDAN

Loving one who doesn't love you is loving the rain that
    falls in the forest.   RUANDA

Your beloved is the object that you love, were it even
    a monkey.   EGYPT

The roots of love are in the heart.	MOROCCO
A man's love goes through his stomach.	
A woman's love goes through her purse.	SOUTH AFRICA
How is one to love a person by being told to love her?	SWAHILI
If anyone loves you he will beg of you.	ASHANTI
One does not love another if one does not accept anything from her.	KANURI
Love has no disputing.	KIKUYU
Don't love me as you do a door, pushed to and fro.	MADAGASCAR
Those who love each other need only a small place.	BUGANDA
Loving one who loves another is a bellyful of trouble.	HAUSA
Be kind to people who love you.	KAONDE
He who loves you wearies you; he who hates you kills you.	MOROCCO
Let your love be like a misty rain, coming softly but flooding the river.	MADAGASCAR
Mutual love is often better than natural brotherhood.	BAKONGO
Love without kisses is not love.	ETHIOPIA
The greatness of love obliterates conventions.	SOTHO
The man who is not jealous in love, loves not.	TAMASHEK
Where there is love there is no darkness.	BURUNDI
He who loves everything dies of it.	BURUNDI
Don't try to make someone hate the person he loves, for he will still go on loving, but he will hate you.	SENEGAL
Love received demands love returned.	MAORI
Everyone in love is the same.	MOROCCO
It is better to be loved than feared.	SENEGAL
He may say that he loves you, wait and see what he does for you.	SENEGAL
Men will love each other as long as one is richer than the other.	UGANDA
Love exceeds reward.	KIKUYU
Love does not hear advice.	GHANA
Love cannot be divided.	KENYA
If you love, love the moon; if you steal, steal a camel.	EGYPT
Love and let the world know, hate in silence.	EGYPT

74

When love comes manners go. TUNISIA

When one is in love, a cliff becomes a meadow. ETHIOPIA

If love is a sickness, patience is the remedy. FULANI

A loved one has no pimples. KENYA

Don't be so much in love that you can't tell when
it's raining. MADAGASCAR

Let your love be like drizzle: it comes softly, but still
swells the river. MADAGASCAR

If love is torn apart you cannot stitch the pieces together
again. MALAGASY

I have spread no snares today
I am caught in my love of you. EGYPT

LOVER

A lover is like a kite—he wants to break the string and fly
to the loved one. MAORI

A lover has no grudge. SWAHILI

A blow from our lover is as sweet as the eating of raisins. EGYPT

The finger must go to the cream;
the lover must join his sweetheart. ZULU

Lovers do not hide their nakedness. CONGO

Lovers are like two turtle doves, always feeding each other. SWAHILI

Love is like being possessed by a spirit; lovers are not their
own masters. ZAIRE

LOVESICK

A lovesick person looks in vain for a doctor.

LOWER

What lowers itself is ready to fall.

LUNACY

There are forty kinds of lunacy, but only one kind of common
sense. BANTU

M

MAID

Even the maid has a family. SOUTH AFRICA

MAN

When a man says he does not mind, then he really does.

When a man says yes, his chi (personal god) says
yes also.

A man who pays respect to the great paves the way for
his own greatness.

You must judge a man by the work of his hands.

If you are threatened by a man, sleep at night, if it is by
a woman then stay awake.

A man is his words. KRU

A man is what he thinks. MALI

A man is a leaf of honey. CAMEROON

Man is like pepper—you only know him when you've
ground him. HAUSA

Man is like palm-wine: when young, sweet but without
strength; in old age, strong but harsh. CONGO

What's too hard for a man must be worth looking into. KENYA

The man who suffers much knows much. HO

No man is complete without marriage. SWAHILI

MAN AND WOMAN

The beauty of a man lies in his intelligence; the intelligence
of a woman lies in her beauty. TUNISIA

I love the man as a standing tree. RUANDA

The folly of a man is not broadcast like that of a woman. CAMEROON

A man finds many faults in a woman when he wants to
divorce, and finds many charms in one's fiancee. MALAGASY

Some men are only strong in their own house—where
they beat their wives. MALAGASY

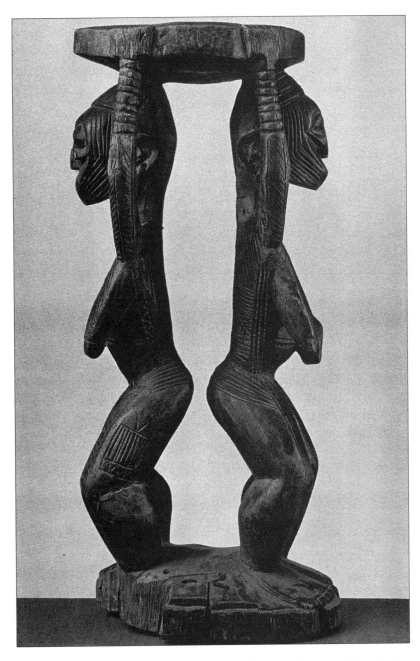

Jukun stool with female figures, from Wukari, Nigeria. Wood, Ht.,
22½ in. Berlin, Museum für Völkerkunde.

The man who travels without his wife will find another on the way. TSONGA

The way of a man following a woman is like footprints in water, they soon vanish. TSONGA

If a woman loves a man she will give it to him even through a hole in a door. MOROCCO

Men fear danger—women only the sight of it. ABYSSINIA

MARKET

The market is not anybody's home. HAUSA

MARKETPLACE

If you haven't been to two marketplaces, you don't know which is the best value. UPPER-VOLTA

MARRIAGE

Let matrimony be like a fowl's clothing, not parted with until death.

Marriage is a snake to slip into your handbag. TSONGA

Marriage is a matter of luck. MASAI

Marriage without good faith is like a teapot without a tray. MOROCCO

If you wish to be blamed, marry; if you wish to be praised, die. GALLA

When one is determined to marry a bad wife, God covers his eyes. IBO

The ties established between two families by a happy marriage are stronger than those of money. TSONGA

Marriage is like a groundnut, you have to crack them to see what is inside. AKAN

If a young woman says no to marriage just wait until her breasts sag. BURUNDI

Marriage is not a tight knot, but a slip knot. MADAGASCAR

Men have thought about their marriage a whole year long—and it lasts but one night. MOORISH

If the wife is unfaithful, the husband is despised. CONGO

Never marry a woman who has bigger feet than you. MOZAMBIQUE

One who marries for love alone will have bad days but good nights. EGYPT

He who marries a beauty marries trouble. NIGER

He never marries who never travels. ZAIRE

Marry a woman of noble birth and sleep on the mat. MOROCCO

Married in a hurry; regretted for life. SOUTH AFRICA

It is Mr. Old-Man-Monkey who marries
Mrs. Old-Woman-Monkey. ASHANTI

MEAT

Meat does not eat meat. NIGERIA

MECCA

Even in Mecca people make money. HAUSA

MEDICINE

Medicine left in the bottle can't help. YORUBA

Healing with medicine is a good thing. MADAGASCAR

The dying man is not saved by medicine. NIGERIA

MEMORY

Memory reaches further than the eyes. KANURI

MESSAGE

He ought to be feared who sends you with a message, not
the one to whom you are sent. MIDWIFE

Whatever the avarice of a midwife, she doesn't come to
the house of a bachelor. HAUSA

MILLET

At the harvest you know how good the millet is. KENYA

MISER

The miser is a thief.

The miser destroys what he collected. EGYPT

MISFORTUNE

The misfortune that comes into town does not wear
a turban. DAHOMEY

Our misfortunes are never out of proportion to our capacity
to bear them. YORUBA

79

Misfortune does not restrict his visits to one day. GHANA

That which brings misfortune is not big. NIGERIA

MODEST

If you are modest, you are modest to your own advantage. YORUBA

An over modest man goes hungry. ETHIOPIA

MONEY

If it hurts to spend your money, you will go hungry.

Money is sharper than a sword. ASHANTI

Better to lose a little money than a little friendship. MADAGASCAR

Abundance of money is a trial for a man. MOROCCO

Everything will satisfy except money; as much as you
have, so much you want. MOROCCO

Money is sweet balm. EGYPT

Making money selling manure is better than losing
money selling musk. EGYPT

Money is like a guest: it comes today, leaves tomorrow. MALAGASY

Love of money is the undoing of men. NIGERIA

Money kills more than do weapons. NIGERIA

MONK

It is easy to become a monk in one's old age. ETHIOPIA

MONKEY

If the monkey reigns, prostrate thyself before him.

I don't sow ground nuts when the monkey is watching.

Only a monkey understands a monkey. SIERRA LEONE

If he keeps on imitating everybody the monkey will one
day cut his own throat. SOUTH AFRICA

The monkey has a big mouth because otherwise he
would be too pretty. EWE

When the monkey can't reach the ripe banana with his
hand, he says it is not sweet. SUDAN

The monkey does not see his own backside; he sees
his neighbor's. ZIMBABWE

When the man is away, the monkey eats his corn and
goes into his hut.   ZULU

The monkey says there is nothing better than poverty to
unlearn man of his conceit.   ASHANTI

By trying often, the monkey learns to jump from the tree.   CAMEROON

Do not dispose of the monkey's tail before he is dead.   CONGO

He who gives a monkey as a present doesn't keep hold of
its tail.   IVORY COAST

A monkey sees its fellow jump and jumps too.   NIGERIA

You do not teach the paths of the forest to an old gorilla.   CONGO

MOON

When the moon is shining the cripple becomes hungry for a walk.

He who waits for the moon waits for darkness.

When the moon is not full, the stars shine more brightly.   BUGANDA

The moon moves slowly, but it gets across the town.   ASHANTI

If the full moon loves you, why worry about the stars?   TUNISIA

If you have the moon, ignore the stars.   MOORISH

No matter how much one is weeping, the moon always
follows the sun.   ETHIOPIA

MORNING

Morning will still come with or without the crowing of
the cock.   BURUNDI

The morning of one's life foreshadows the eve.   YORUBA

The darkness of night cannot stop the light of morning.   CAMEROON

MOSQUITO

Do not be like the mosquito that bites the owner of
the house.   MALAWI

The mosquito is small—but when he sings, your ears are
full of him.   MAURITIUS

A fig tree with figs turned out to be a ruin with
mosquitoes.   MOROCCO

Their mosquito won't bite me.   IVORY COAST

When mosquitoes work, they bite and then they sing.   MALI

Mother

He whose mother is naked is not likely to clothe his aunt.

The source of human love is the mother. BAKONGO

The mother is she who catches the knife by the blade. BOTSWANA

Mother is gold. YORUBA

No one will sympathize with one as much as one's own mother; for, who will show kindness to another person's child? YORUBA

A child who has a mother eats a second time. BONDEI

There is no mother like your own mother. BAMBARA

A mother's wrath does not survive the night. BURUNDI

After I saw what my mother did, I will never trust a widow. TUNISIA

As your mother has advised you, so has our mother advised us, too. GHANA

Only a mother would carry the child that bites. NIGERIA

A mother is gold, a father is a mirror. NIGERIA

More than one mother can make tasty soup. NIGERIA

Mother-in-Law

If you laugh at your mother-in-law you'll get dirt in your eye. SWAHILI

The mother-in-law shows you her thighs without shame, you are the embarrassed one. CONGO

Mothers-in-law are hard of hearing. CONGO

Woe to the high spirited bride whose mother-in-law is still alive. ZAIRE

Mouse

As long as the mouse keeps still you can be sure that the cat stays on guard. MADAGASCAR

Mouth

The mouth which eats does not talk.

When the mouth stumbles, it is worse than the foot.

What comes out of the mouth has lost its master. GABON

"Mr. Mouth" hurt his master. YAO

Mouth not keeping to mouth and lip not keeping to lip, bring trouble to the jaws. YORUBA

Let the heart be overflowing, but let the mouth be restrained.   EGYPT

Open your mouth before you eat.   MAURITANIA

If you put a razor in your mouth, you will spit blood.   NIGERIA

MOVING

Each one has his own way of moving.   KENYA

MULE

They asked the mule who his father was, he said my uncle
is the horse.   TUNISIA

MURDER

If you want to get at the root of murder . . . you have to
look for the blacksmith who made the hatchet.   EWE

MUSIC

Move your neck according to the music.   ETHIOPIA

NAKED

A naked man will often laugh at someone with torn clothes.   SUDAN

He who is covered with other people's clothes is naked.   TUNISIA

NECESSITY

He who has the necessities has no shame.

NEEDLE

A needle cannot hold two threads or a mind two thoughts.

It is the path of the needle that the thread is accustomed
to follow.

The point of the needle must pass first.   ETHIOPIA

When a needle falls into a deep well, many people will look
into the well, but few will be ready to go down after it.   GUINEA

83

NEIGHBOUR

We can do without our friends, but not our neighbours.   EGYPT

A good deed will make a good neighbour.   BANTU

Do not mend your neighbour's fence before seeing to
your own.   TANZANIA

I am talking to you, daughter-in-law, so that you could
hear it, neighbour!   EGYPT

Be patient with a bad neighbour: he may move or face
misfortune.   EGYPT

Choose your neighbours before you buy your house.   HAUSA

It's easy to weed your neighbour's field.   NAMIBIA

The head of your neighbour is a kingdom and his heart
a wood.   NIGERIA

Your neighbour's wife cannot make you grow up.   TETELA

NEW

The new pleases and the old satisfies.   GHANA

NEWS

News does not sleep on the way.

NIGHT

The words of the night are coated with butter; as soon as
the sun shines they melt away.

Even the night has ears.   TANZANIA

The night is the king of the shadows.   SENEGAL

He who spends a night with a chicken will cackle in the
morning.   TUNISIA

No matter how long the night, the day is sure to come.   ZAIRE

He who does not lose his way by night will not lose his way
by day.   HAUSA

He who led me in the night, will be thanked by me at
daybreak.   MOZAMBIQUE

NILE

If the Nile knows your secret it will soon be in the desert.   AMHARIC

Cover up the good you do—do like the Nile and conceal
your sources.   EGYPT

Don't demand that what you write in the Nile will be read in
the desert. ETHIOPIA

No

Say 'no' from the start; you will have rest.

Nut

Don't despise the nut, one day it will be a palm tree. ANGOLA

The nuts from a palm tree don't fall without dragging a few
leaves with it. ZAIRE

Old Age

Old age does not announce itself. ZULU

There is no medicine against old age. YORUBA

Old age devours your youth. KENYA

When you get older you keep warm with the wood you
gathered as a youth. BAMBARA

When there are no old men, the town is ruined. YORUBA

Any old pole will find a hole in the fence. IBO

Old Man

Where there is an old man, one doesn't ask the advice of
a young man. HO

Where there is an old man nothing need go wrong. SWAHILI

If you see and old man running, either he is chasing
something or something is chasing him. NUPE

Even though the old man is strong and hearty, he will not
live forever. ASHANTI

The child looks everywhere and often sees nought; but the
old man sitting on the ground sees everything. SENEGAL

ONE-EYED MAN

The one-eyed man thanks God only when he sees a man
   blind in both eyes.   NIGERIA

ONION

An onion offered with love is worth a sheep.   EGYPT

ORANGE

An orange never bears a lime.   SIERRA LEONE

OTHERS

Through others I am somebody.

P

PALM-KERNELS

Those whose palm-kernels were cracked for them by a
   benevolent spirit should not forget to be humble.

PANTHER

If the panther knew how much he is feared, he would do
   much more harm.   CAMEROON
The panther and the sheep never hunt together.   IVORY COAST

PARADISE

Paradise is open at the command of mothers.
Without human companions, paradise itself would be an
   undesirable place.

PARASITE

A parasite cannot live alone.   NAMIBIA

PARTNERSHIP

If there is any profit in partnership, two will share a woman.   TUNISIA
A partner in the business will not put an obstacle to it.   ETHIOPIA

Partridge

The last partridge will take the most arrows.

Patience

Live patiently in the world; know that those who hate you
    are more numerous than those who love you.

Patience is the mother of a beautiful child.   Bantu

The patient one becomes the victor.   Toucouleure

To the patient man will come all the riches of the world.   Liberia

The patient man cooks a stone till he drinks broth from it.   Hausa

At the bottom of patience there is heaven.   Kanuri

In the gate of patience there is no crowding.   Morocco

Peace

If you want peace in the house, do what your wife wants.

Peace is costly, but it's worth the expense.   Baguirmi

Pearl

Those who wear pearls do not know how often the shark
    bites the leg of the diver.

Pebble

One pebble doesn't make a floor.   Hausa

Penis

A large penis is not manhood.   Ovambo

A small penis can beget a child.   Ovambo

When the penis beholds the vulva it rises.   Ibo

What effects the penis, effects the vagina.   Ibo

People

We are people because of other people.   Sotho

Phrase

There is no phrase that doesn't have a double meaning.   Kenya

Piety

Singing 'Halleluia' everywhere does not prove piety.   Ethiopia

PIG

A pig that is used to swallowing in the dirt looks for a clean
person to rub against.   NIGERIA

You can't stop a pig from wallowing in the mud.   YORUBA

PLEASE

Blessed are those who can please themselves.   ZULU

POET

Slowly but surely the excrement of foreign poets will come
to your village.   MALI

POLITENESS

Learn politeness from the impolite.   EGYPT

POLYGAMIST

The polygamist will love the latest wife.   KAONDE

POOL

A little pool without water! Yet men drown in it.   NIGER

A small deep pool of water will exhaust the breath.   MAORI

POOR

People think that the poor are not so wise as the rich, for
if a man be wise, why is he poor?

When the poor man sets a trap only his dog gets caught.   CAMEROON

The poor are excused from washing with soap.   SUDAN

Three kinds of people die poor: those who divorce, those
who incur debts, and those who move around too much. SENEGAL

The efforts of the poor are their tears.   EGYPT

A poor man is a snake—his brothers avoid him because of
the misery of the poverty stricken.   ZANZIBAR

A poor man's sheep will never get fat.   IVORY COAST

PORCUPINE

One should never rub bottoms with a porcupine.   AKAN

POSSESSIONS

When your own possessions are gone, those of another
   are of little use.   NIGERIA

What a person possesses is not stronger than him or
   herself.   KANURI

POT

Every pot will find its top.   SWAHILI

POTTER

The potter eats from broken plates.

POVERTY

Poverty without debt is real wealth.

Poverty is an older daughter of laziness.   PEUL

Poverty is slavery.   SOMALIA

POWER

If power can be bought then sell your mother to get it.
   You can always buy her back later.   GHANA

Those in power never give way and admit defeat. They plot
   and scheme to regain their lost power and privilege.   EGYPT

PRAISE

If you praise the man who taps the palm tree, he'll put water
   in the palm wine.   ZANZIBAR

PRAYER

The prayer of the innocent has no wings.   BERBER

Everything is formed by habit, even praying.   EGYPT

PREGNANT

Pregnancy and fire cannot be kept secret.   RUANDA BURUNDI

A pregnant woman is not afraid if you threaten her with
   what you made her pregnant with.   BAMBARA

The pregnant woman can't see her belly.   IVORY COAST

89

PRIDE

Pride only goes as far as one can spit. BAKONGO

Pride and dignity would belong to women if only men
would leave them alone. EGYPT

PROFIT

Accomplishment of purpose is better than making a profit. HAUSA

PROMISE

A promise is a debt. SWAHILI

Evening promises are like butter: morning comes, and it's
all melted. MOROCCO

PROSTITUTE

The prostitute can make you useless. MASAI

PURSE

You are worth as much as your purse. BERBER

A blow to another's purse is like a blow to a mountain
of sand. EGYPT

Bajokwe comb, Kasai region, Belgian Congo. Wood. Tervueren, Musée Royal du Congo Belge.

Quarrel

The quarrel that doesn't concern you is pleasant to hear about.   HAUSA

Quarrels end, but words once spoken never die.   SIERRA LEONE

Even Buddhist priests of the same temple quarrel occasionally.   SENEGAL

If you tell people to live together, you tell them to quarrel.   ZAIRE

If a man quarrels with corn, hunger will kill him.   HAUSA

Every tree has a thick end, and every quarrel has a cause.   NIGERIA

Quarrel is not a food which is eaten.   GHANA

With man comes the quarrel.   ETHIOPIA

Question

He who asks questions, cannot avoid the answers.   CAMEROON

R

Rags

Your own rags are better than another's gown. HAUSA

Rain

It rained on the mountaintop, but it was the valley below
    that got flooded.

Rain does not fall on one roof alone. CAMEROON

Help from abroad always comes when the rain has
    stopped. RUANDA BURUNDI

Raisin

Every raisin contains a pip. LIBYA

Rat

The rat cannot call the cat to account. NIGER

The witness of a rat is another rat. ETHIOPIA

Let rats shoot arrows at each other. SUDAN

You set the trap when the rat has gone. RUANDA BURUNDI

Razor

A razor may be sharper than an axe, but it cannot cut wood.

Reception

The reception has more value than the invitation. BURUNDI

Reflection

A reflection does not see itself.

Regret

Regret, like a tail, comes at the end. ABYSSINIA

Relations

Relations are scorpions. TUNISIAN

RELATIVES

Relatives are like a part of our body; if anything touches it,
however small, you feel it.   HAUSA

If relatives help each other, what harm can be done
to them?   ETHIOPIA

If you have no relatives get married.   EGYPT

REPETITION

Repetition is the mother of knowledge.

RESPECT

Respect depends on reciprocity.   NYANG

Whoever does not respect you, insults you.   MOROCCO

REVENGE

To take revenge is often to sacrifice oneself.   BAKONGO

RHINOCEROS

Do not talk about a rhinoceros if there is no tree nearby.   ZULU

RICE

Sweet rice is eaten quickly.   SIERRA LEONE

RICH

If you get rich, be in a dark corner when you jump for joy.

The rich are always complaining.   ZULU

A rich person is seldom condemned, for the mouth which
eats another's property is benumbed.   IBO

One cannot both feast and become rich.   ASHANTI

There is no one who became rich because he broke a
holiday, and no one who became fat because he broke
a fast.   ETHIOPIA

A rich man is allowed to wear old clothes.   GHANA

The rich man never dances badly.   RUANDA BURUNDI

The richest of men is he who fills his coffers with love.   MOROCCO

Rich and Poor

If a rich man asks for children, dollars come to him, and
   if a poor man asks for dollars, children come to him.   Morocco

The poor man and the rich man do not play together.   Ashanti

When you are rich, you are resented; when you are poor,
   you are despised.   Ashanti

If a rich man steals it is a mistake; if a poor man makes
   a mistake he has stolen.   Morocco

River

No matter how full the river, it still wants to swell more.   Zaire

You cannot cross a river without getting wet.   Zulu

A little rain each day will fill the rivers to overflowing.   Liberia

The river may dry up but she keeps her name.   Nigeria

Rope

If he gives you a rope, tie him with it.   Tunisia

Put a rope around your neck and many will be happy to
   drag you along.   Egypt

Rose

For the sake of the rose the thorn is watered too.

Round

All that is round is not a cake.   Libya

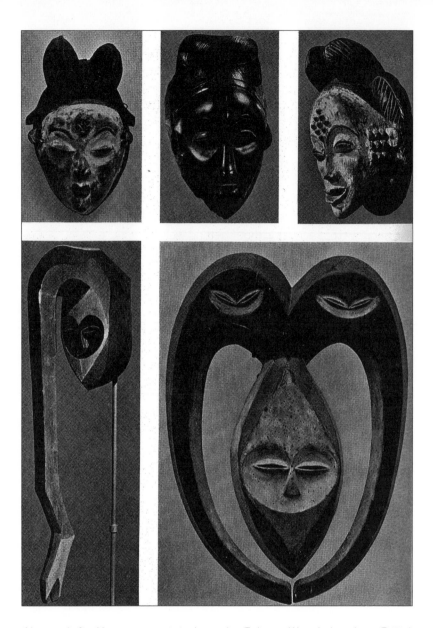

Above, left: *Mpongwe painted mask, Gabon. Wood. London, British Museum.* Center: *Mpongwe mask. Wood. Brussels, Coll. Schwob.* Right: *Balumbo painted mask, Gabon. Wood.* Below: *Bakwele painted masks, Middle Congo. Wood. Last three objects, New York, Museum of Primitive Art.*

S

Sadness

Sadness is a valuable treasure—only discovered in people
    you love. MALAGASY

Salt

A load of salt on another man's head is easily carried.

Don't buy the salt if you haven't licked it yet. ZAIRE

Sand

A building of sand falls as you build it. FULANI

Scandal

Scandal is like an egg; when it is hatched it has wings.

Scratch

Only scratch where you can reach. KENYA

Sea

Smooth seas do not make skillful sailors.

Secret

Your secret is your blood—when you shed it you die. BERBER

Sharing a secret with a rogue is like carrying grain in a bag
    with a hole. ETHIOPIA

Seduce

I am not a snake which kills its prey and leaves it. I have
    killed to eat—I have seduced the girl but also want to
    marry her. TSONGA

See

Seeing is different from being told. KENYA

Seeing is better than hearing. NIGERIA

Distracted by what is far away, he does not see his nose. MALAGASY

SEED

Don't plant a seed in the sea.   SWAHILI

The seed waits for the garden where it will be sown.   ZULU

If all seeds that fall were to grow, then no one could follow
the path under the trees.   AKAN

SERVANT

The heart of a servant that is not beaten is full of curses.   EGYPT

SEX

Youths have changed the usual sex habit.   IBO

Don't uncover a woman for sex and dish out a slap.   IBO

Hurrying over sex, prevents "the Journey" from moving
as expected.   IBO

Much sleep with a woman produces blindness.   MOROCCA

If you do not sleep with a woman in the morning she will
not become pregnant.   OVAMBO

You cannot produce one human being without uniting
two bodies.   CAMEROON

SHADOW

However swift a man, he will not outstrip his shadow.   FULANI

SHAME

Shame has watchmen.   ZIMBABWE

He who knows not shame does whatever he likes.   EGYPT

Where there is no shame, there is no honor.   ETHIOPIA

Nobody is shamed twice.   GOLD COAST

SHAVE

He who does not shave you does not cut you.   SOMALIA

You cannot shave a man's head in his absence.   YORUBA

SHEEP

The quarrel of the sheep doesn't concern the goats.

A sheep cannot bleat in two different places at the
same time.   TANZANIA

'O, sheep if I do not eat you, you will eat me',
    said the hyena.   Ethiopia

In the villages where there are no oxen, the sheep's
    feet seem strong.   Ivory Coast

Shoes

Before you buy shoes, measure your feet.

If you are wearing shoes, you don't fear the thorns.   Sudan

He who travels with gold shoes may reach the world's end.   Amharic

Sickness

Sickness comes with a waning moon; a new moon cures
    disease.   Le Sotho

To a physician a sick man is a garden.   Swahili

One who recovers from sickness, forgets about God.   Ethiopia

If you want to give a sick man medicine, let him first be
    really ill—so that he can see how well the medicine works.   Nigeria

He who is sick will not refuse medicine.   Nigeria

When you are sick you promise a goat, but when well again,
    you make do with a chicken.   Nigeria

Annoy your doctor and sickness comes in laughing.   Rhodesia

He who conceals his disease cannot expect to be cured. Ethiopia

Silence

Silence produces peace and peace produces safety.   Swahili

Silence is also speech.   Fulfulde

Silence is the door of consent.   Berber

Silence is the best answer to the stupid.   Egypt

Silence is more than just a lack of words.   Egypt

Sit

Sitting is being crippled.   Ethiopia

Skin

One rolls up a skin while it is still damp.   Tsonga

Rain beats on a leopard's skin, but it does not wash out
    the spots.   Ashanti

Skinny

Hit him with a bean, he will break   Tunisia

Slander

Slander by the stream will be heard by the frogs.   Mozambique

Slave

A slave has no choice.   Kenya

When a slave mounts a camel he wants to ride on both
    humps.   Egypt

A slave does not choose his master.   Ashanti

A slave's wisdom is in his master's head.   Ghana

The person who has been a slave from birth does not
    value rebellion.   Yoruba

Sleep

Sleep is as powerful as a sultan.   Egypt

Sleep is the cousin of death.   Congo

He who cannot sleep can still dream.   Ivory Coast

Slowness

Slowness comes from God and quickness from the devil.   Morocco

Small Matters

Small matters breed important ones.

Smile

Smile . . . heaven is watching!

The teeth are smiling, but is the heart?   Zaire

A smiling face dispels unhappiness.   Hausa

Smoke

He who cultivates in secret is betrayed by the smoke.   Chagga

Smoke rises from beneath every roof.   Bambara

A single stick may smoke, but it will not burn.   Ethiopia

Snail

The snail leaves its trail wherever it goes.

SNAKE

The son of a snake is a snake.

He who takes a light to find a snake should start at his own feet.

Although the snake does not fly it has caught the bird whose home is in the sky. AKAN

One little arrow does not kill a serpent. MALAWI

When you chop off a snake's head all you are left with is a piece of rope. BAMBARA

He who is bitten by a snake fears a lizard. BUGANDA

The snake and the crab don't sleep in the same hole. CONGO

Do not walk into a snake-pit with your eyes open. SOMALIA

Snake at your feet—a stick at your hand! ETHIOPIA

One doesn't throw the stick after the snake has gone. LIBERIA

A snake that you can see does not bite. MOZAMBIQUE

Because we focused on the snake, we missed the scorpion. EGYPT

Restless feet may walk into a snake pit. ETHIOPIA

SON

The son shoots a leopard; the father is proud. ZAIRE

A bad son gives his mother a bad name. IVORY COAST

SORROW

Sorrow is like a precious treasure, shown only to friends. MADAGASCAR

Sorrow doesn't kill—reckless joy does. YORUBA

SOUP

The soup would be none the worse for more meat. SUDAN

SPARROW

The sparrow says: 'I have not eaten . . . so the parrot will not eat either.'

SPEAK

Who speaks alone is always right. ZANZIBAR

Eat when the meal is ready, speak when the time is ripe. ETHIOPIA

101

SPOON

He who has no spoon will burn his hands. MAURITANIA

SPOUSE

A person without a spouse is like a vase without
flowers. CAPE VERDE ISLANDS

Many are the eyes of the person whose spouse commits
adultery. BEMBA

SPRING

The spring makes the stream flow.

No matter how long the winter, spring is sure to follow. GUINEA

STAND

Standing is still going. SWAHILI

STOMACH

What is in the stomach carries what is in the head.

There is no god like one's stomach;
We must sacrifice to it every day. YORUBA

A full stomach is a snare, you go on and are in want. TUMBULCA

He whose stomach is empty is evil and becomes an
opponent and grumbler. EGYPT

If the stomach-ache were in the foot, one would go lame. NIGERIA

STONE

The thrower of stones throws away the strength of his
own arm.

Who throws stones at night, kills his own brother. DAHOMEY

If someone hits you with a stone, hit him with bread; your
bread will return to you and his stone will return to him. TUNISIA

The land where the stones know you is worth more than
the land where the people know you. BERBER

If a blind man says let's throw stones, be assured that
he has stepped on one. HAUSA

The stone in the water does not know how hot the hill is,
parched by the sun. NIGERIA

STORY

If you want to know the true story, wait till the arguments start.

An old story does not open the ear as a new one does. YORUBA

STRANGER

The stranger has big eyes but he doesn't see anything. IVORY COAST

When a stranger is hungry he sleeps, but when he has eaten his fill he goes about accosting the town folks' wives. ASHANTI

STRATEGY

Strategy is better than strength. HAUSA

STRENGTH

Strength does not prevent a man from dying. KIKUYU

Hurrying and worrying are not the same as strength. HAUSA

The strong don't need clubs. SENEGAL

SUBTLENESS

A little subtleness is better than a lot of force. CONGO

SUCCESS

The success of a man is through the soles of his feet, that of a woman is from her legs.

The sun will shine on those who stand before it shines on those who kneel.

SUN

Midday sun is the remedy for a cold. HAUSA

The little stars will always shine while the great sun is often eclipsed. ABYSSINIA

How lovely is the sun after rain, and how lovely is laughter after sorrow. TUNISIA

The eye of the sun can't be hidden. EGYPT

No dew ever competed with the sun. ZULU

SURE

He who is too sure of himself and acts without thinking is
    heading for his downfall.

SWEETNESS

If sweetness be excessive, it is no longer sweetness.

Sweetness eats up itself.   KIKUYU

SWIM

Ability to swim is preservation of life.   HAUSA

T

TALK

People should not talk while they are eating or pepper
    may go down the wrong way.

He who talks incessantly, talks nonsense.   IVORY COAST

Talking to one another is loving one another.   KENYA

One must talk little, and listen a lot.   MAURITANIA

There is none quick of speech who is free of hasty words
    and none light of heart and mind whose thoughts
    have weight.   EGYPT

Do not say the first thing that comes to your mind.   KENYA

Why keep on talking when we know you so well?   NIGERIA

TATTOO

No tattoo is made without blood.   MOZAMBIQUE

TEARS

If a man makes soup of his tears, ask him not for broth.

Nothing wipes your tears away but your own hand.

Stool with supporting female figure. Baluba style, Kasai region, Belgian Congo. Wood. Antwerp, Ethnografisch Museum.

TERMITE

Small termites collapse the roof.

Termites live underground. ETHIOPIA

A termite can do nothing to a stone save lick it. SUDAN

THIEF

A thief does not like to be robbed. BANTU

A thief is always under suspicion. SOMALIA

When a thief finds nothing to steal he will steal a dagger
made of sand. BERBER

A good thief is the best guardian. GUYANA

One cry of 'Thief' and the whole marketplace is on the l
ookout. HAUSA

Grass does not grow on the nose of a thief. NIGERIA

THIGHS

It is inevitable that two thighs will rub against each other. ZAMBIA

THORN

A man does not run among thorns for no reason; either he
is chasing a snake or a snake is chasing him.

Thorns themselves will not harm you—you hurt yourself on
the thorns.

THOUGHT

Thought breaks the heart. CAMEROON

As the wound inflames the finger, so the thought inflames
the mind. ETHIOPIA

If everyone thought alike, no goods would ever be sold. LIBYA

THUNDER

Thunder is not yet rain. KENYA

A deaf man may not have heard the thunder but he surely
will see the rain. MALI

TIGER

A tiger does not have to proclaim its tigritude. NIGERIA

TIME

Time destroys all things. NIGERIA

All the world fears time, but time fears the Pyramids. EGYPT

Do not waste your time looking for soft ground to drive your
spade in. MALAGASY

No man rules forever on the throne of time. GHANA

TOAD

The toad likes water, but not when it's boiling. GUINEA

TOMORROW

When you wait for tomorrow it never comes. When you don't
wait for it tomorrow still comes. GUINEA

TONGUE

If you take your tongue to the pawnshop, you can't redeem
it later. ASHANTI

Beautify your tongue, you will attain what you desire. MOROCCO

A good tongue meeting another good tongue will cause
happiness. CONGO

TOOTH

A loose tooth will not rest until it's pulled out. ETHIOPIA

The teeth that laugh are also those that bite. HAUSA

If you are not going to bite, don't show your teeth. IVORY COAST

Teeth will never quarrel with the tongue. IVORY COAST

TORTOISE

When you invite a tortoise to a meal it is no use giving
him water to wash his paws, because he will soon walk
on the ground and dirty them.

TOWN

The town is a barren wilderness to one who is unhappy
in one's homelife. YORUBA

The one who is carried does not realize how far away the
town is. NIGERIA

If the townspeople are happy, look for the cook. LIBERIA

107

TRADE

Because he has so many trades, he is unemployed.   TUNISIA

TRAVEL

Travel and you will see them, sit and they will come to you.

The wise traveler leaves his heart at home.

A traveler with a tongue doesn't lose his way.

If you are planning to travel where corn grows, you should
take a sickle with you.   ABYSSINIA

You travel on until you return home; you live on until you
return to earth.   ABYSSINIA

The road doesn't tell the traveller what lies ahead.   BANTU

If you do not travel, you will marry your own sister.   MOZAMBIQUE

Someone else's legs are no good to you when you're
travelling.   NIGERIA

He who has travelled alone can tell what he likes.   RUANDA BURUNDI

He who travels with gold shoes may reach the world's end.   ETHIOPIA

Making preparations does not spoil the trip.   GUINEA

He who doesn't know the road holds back the one who does.   KIKUYU

The day you are leaving is not the time to start your
preparations.   NIGERIA

TREE

The tree that is not taller than you cannot shade you.

The tree breaks that takes the force of the wind.

A tree that grows in the shade of another one, will die small.   SENEGAL

The tree with the sweetest fruit is guarded by demons.   NKUNDA

If you climb up a tree, you must climb down the
same tree.   SIERRA LEONE

A little shrub may grow into a tree.   SUDAN

Even the mightest eagle comes down to the tree tops
to rest.   UGANDA

An ugly tree may yield sweet sap.   NAMIBIA

Mock the palm tree only when the date harvest is over.   ABYSSINIA

The best trees grow on the steepest hills.   BURUNDI

You may well have two legs but you still can't climb two trees at the same time. ETHIOPIA

You cannot climb a tree with one hand. GABON

Around a flowering tree, there are many insects. GUINEA

If a dead tree falls, it carries with it a live one. KENYA

Though the palm tree in the jungle is big, who knows how big its yield will be? LIBERIA

Only when the tree is big and strong can you tether a cow to it. LIBERIA

Do not measure up the wood before the tree is cut down. MALAGASY

Not all the tree's blossoms will bear fruit. MAURITANIA

On a dead tree there are no monkeys. MOZAMBIQUE

You can't jump from one tree to another but you can from one man to another. NIGERIA

TROUBLE

To trouble me is better than to forget me.

A man who creates trouble seldom eats it himself. BANTU

TRUTH

Truth and morning become light with time. ETHIOPIA

The voice of truth is easily known. WOLOF

The word of a powerful man is the truth. BAMBARA

Truth came to market but could not be sold; however, we buy lies with ready cash. YORUBA

The truth is like gold: keep it locked up and you will find it exactly as you first put it away. SENEGAL

Truth keeps the hand cleaner than soap. NIGERIA

Over truth there is light. MOROCCO

TURTLE

A turtle is not proud of his long neck. MALI

TWIG

The twig that falls in the water will never become a fish. IVORY COAST

Two

Two is good, one alone cannot wash his back.

Tyrant

The tyrant is only the slave turned inside out.

EGYPT

U

UGLY

An old rice bag is ugly, but the thing inside is beautiful.   KPELLE

If there is character ugliness becomes beauty, if there is
    none beauty becomes ugliness.   NIGERIA

Ugliness with a good character is better than beauty.   HAUSA

If you are ugly, be winsome.   TUNISIA

If you are ugly, know how to dance.   ZAMBIA

UPSET

He who upsets something should know how to put it
    back again.   SIERRA LEONE

V

VASE

He who loves the vase loves also what is inside.

VINE

When the vine entwines your roof, it is time to cut it down.   CAMEROON

VIPER

The viper assumes the colours of his surroundings.

VIRTUE

Virtue is power.   KIKUYU

Virtue is better than wealth.   KENYA

The sin for which you repent is the father of virtue; but a
    virtue that you talk about, is the mother of sin.   MALAGASY

Basonge shield, painted in blue and gray, decorated with a mask, Katanga region, Belgian Congo. Wood. Brussels, Coll. Schwob.

W

Walk

Who cannot yet walk, cannot climb a ladder.   ETHIOPIA

War

Nobody wages war with ghosts.

War ends nothing.   ZAIRE

Without war there can be no peace.   CONGO

You cannot wage war without the sound of gunpowder.   MALI

We come to a party to show teeth.

We go to war to show our arms.   LIBERIA

Water

Where water is the boss, there the land must obey.

Water is never tired of flowing.

The water can only flow thanks to the well.

Return to old watering holes for more than water; friends
    and dreams are there to meet you.

Water always finds a way out.   CAMEROON

Water is the king of food.   KANURI

Spilled water is better than a broken jar.   SENEGAL

It is only the water that is spilled; the bowl is not broken!   MAURITANIA

In the ocean, one does not need to sow water.   SOMALIA

Water and milk do not mix.   SOMALIA

Dirty water cannot be washed.   TOGO

The watercarrier does not drink mud.   TOGO

Prepare yourself before the water comes up to your knees.   ZAIRE

The surface of the water is beautiful, but it is no good to
    sleep on.   ASHANTI

It is the calm and silent water that drowns a man.   ASHANTI

Boil the water and the scum will rise to the top.   BERBER

Taking water from the same well doesn't make all the wives'
    gravy taste good.   IVORY COAST

The water of the river flows on without waiting for the
thirsty man. KENYA

Water in a jar doesn't become milk. EGYPT

Warm water never forgets that it was once cold. NIGERIA

WEALTH

Where there is no wealth there is no poverty.

There is no wealth where there are no children. JABO

A wealthy man will always have followers. NIGERIA

Wealth is like hair in nose: it hurts to be separated whether
from a little or from a lot. MALAGASY

A man's wealth may be superior to him. CAMEROON

Wealth is bits of roasted meat. The great thing is one's
kith and kin. TSONGA

Wealth diminishes with usage; learning increases with use. ZANZIBAR

Trusting in wealth is like looking for feathers on turtles. SENEGAL

The wealth of the wicked will be scattered by the wind
like chaff. MOZAMBIQUE

With wealth one wins a woman. UGANDA

One cannot count on riches. SOMALIA

WELL

They who dig the wells never drink from them.

WHITE MAN

As long as the white man stutters, the interpreters have a
lot of work.

The white man never forgets Europe. CONGO

The white man lives in the castle; when he dies, he lies in
the ground. ASHANTI

When the white man is about to leave the garden for good,
he wrecks it. YORUBA

WIDOW

You flirt with a widow, but do you know how her husband died? TOGO

'I won't tie up the mule in a horse's stall,' says the widow. BERBER

WIFE

If you have five wives, then you have five tongues.

Differences between husband and wife should not be aired
    in the marketplace.

A wife is like a giant. GA

One wife one eye. OVAMBO

One who is looking for a wife does not speak contemptuously
    of a woman. ASHANTI

What happens to your wife happens to yourself. MADAGASCAR

It is the wife who knows her husband. ASHANTI

Better a stupid wife than a mess at home. TOGO

The idiot who has his eye on your wife is like a blood
    sucking fly. EGYPT

Two wives would have been fun, but it is hot fire and sweat. IBO

Whoever is ashamed to sleep with his wife will never have
    children. EGYPT

A wife who has left one husband may leave you too. MASAI

Because he killed his wife he took shelter with his in-laws. ETHIOPIA

Lying will get you a wife, but it won't keep her. FULANI

The man with one wife is the boss of all bachelors. UGANDA

Take away the wife of a strong man only when he is out. UGANDA

If you want to know what your wife will look when she gets
    old, look at your mother-in-law. CAMEROON

Better a bad wife than an empty house. IVORY COAST

WILDERNESS

The wilderness has ears. KAMBA

WINE

He who is drunk from wine can sober up, he who is drunk
    from wealth cannot.

If you don't live near a wine palm you won't be tempted to
    drink palm wine.

WINK

If you don't understand it with a wink, you certainly will
    with a blow. MOROCCO

WISDOM

Wisdom does not come overnight. SOMALIA

Wisdom is not a medicine to be swallowed. BAKONGO

The wisdom of this year is the folly of the next. YORUBA

The breaking day has wisdom, the falling day, experience. NDANGA

WISE

The wise man is father of the fool.

The heart of a fool is in his mouth and the mouth of the
wise man is in his heart. ABYSSINIA

The heart of the wise man lies quiet like limpid water. CAMEROON

The appearance of the wise differs from that of the fool. YORUBA

WITCH DOCTOR

Witch doctors do not sell their potions to each other. MOZAMBIQUE

WOLF

The wolf dies where the pack is. SENEGAL

WOMAN

A woman is like a banana; one can turn the whole bunch rotten.

A woman's strength is a multitude of words.

Woman is king. SUDAN

Buy all the presents you will, if a woman does not love you,
she is bound to marry another. NIGERIA

If a woman is beautiful she will have many faults. ZIGULA

When a beautiful woman does not steal, she takes you. BURKINO FASO

Quickly loving a woman means quickly not loving a woman. YORUBA

Against the goodness of woman the sadness of man is
also good. ETHIOPIA

A house may hold a hundred men, but the heart of a woman
has only room for one of them. EGYPT

You need double strength if you quarrel with a woman whose
husband is absent. SHONA

Women are the devil's traps. SOMALIA

He who doesn't like chattering women must stay a bachelor. CONGO

117

If a woman sees the stick for beating her rival, she will throw it away in the wood. UGANDA

Do not insult a woman before she has undressed. ZAMBIA

A woman is like the milk of a young coconut; not very nice—save in the shell. ZANZIBAR

Women are attractive when they marry someone else. ZIMBABWE

A woman is like a blanket—if you cover yourself with it, it bothers you; if you throw it aside you will feel the cold. ASHANTI

With tender words you have less luck with a woman than with jewels. BERBER

Better to kiss an ugly woman than to lick yourself. BURUNDI

The woman who does not covet the possessions of her husband is in love with another man. EGYPT

A woman of high birth can drive her husband away and take another, but she cannot marry both at the same time. OVAMBO

A woman who calls her husband "father" is carrying her esteem for him too far. YORUBA

When a woman is not singing, she is not working much either. EGYPT

A woman will be twice bound when her chains feel comfortable. EGYPT

Woman without man is like a field without seed. ETHIOPIA

If a woman gets rich she changes into a man. GHANA

Only believe a woman one day later. KENYA

Divorce a young woman and you make another man happy. MALAGASY

A woman who offers sex to everyone will get kicked by everyone. MALI

Women know ninety nine tricks and even Satan doesn't know the hundredth. NIGERIA

The advice of a woman ends with 'Oh, if I had only known!' NIGERIA

A woman who is not successful in her own marriage, has no advice for her younger generations. NIGERIA

A woman who admits her guilt doesn't spend too much time on her knees. NIGERIA

The woman is cold water that kills you; deep water that you drown in. NIGERIA

A woman who has not been twice married cannot know
what a perfect marriage is. NIGERIA

Women are like one's shadow. They follow at the heels of
those who run away from them. They bully and boss and
lead those who follow them. SOMALIA

Desire for a woman took hold of me in the night like
madness. AZANDE

She is like a road—pretty, but crooked. CAMEROON

If I have a headache, I have myself bled.
If I have a colic, I take some medicine.
If I am seized by the pox, I go down to the hot springs.
But where is there help, for what she does to me? ETHIOPIA

WOOD

A piece of wood that has been burned easily catches fire. TOGO

WORDS

Words form a hard knot that never rots. KRU

The poison of a word is a word. SWAHILI

Too many words black your ears. BURUNDI

Great events may stem from words of no importance. CONGO

A man with two ears can be supported by two words. EGYPT

Even the best words bring no food. GAMBIA

Words are like the spider's web—a shelter for the clever
ones and a trap for the not-so-clever. MALAGASY

Words are like newly hatched eggs—they already
have wings. MALAGASY

Words go further than bullets. MALAGASY

A cutting word is worse than a bowstring; a cut may heal,
but the cut of the tongue does not. MAURITANIA

It is worse to be wounded by words than a sword. MOROCCO

WORK

Work is the medicine for poverty. YORUBA

It is work that puts one man ahead of another. NUPE

It is no shame at all to work for money. ASHANTI

Work is good provided you do not forget to live. BANTU

Peanut-pounding board. Art of Bush Negroes. Evanston, Ill., M. J. and F. S. Herskovits Coll.

Whenever I work hard for other people, I always sleep on
an empty stomach. BANTU

It is better to work and be free than to be fed in captivity. GABON

Work and you will be strong; sit and you will smell. MOROCCO

Voluntary work is better than slavery. NIGERIA

A person always breaking off from work never finishes
anything. NIGERIA

WORLD

The world has not made a promise to anybody.

This world is a harsh place, this world. ZULU

In the world all things are two and two. TANZANIA

WOUND

A person with a wound on his head keeps touching it. EGYPT

WRITTEN

That which is written is binding, but that which is spoken is
forgotten. AMHARIC

WRONGDOER

The wrongdoer forgets, but not the wronged.

Let a wrong doing repeat itself at least three times: the first
may be an accident, the second a mistake, but the third is
likely to be intentional. ABYSSINIA

YES

The word 'yes' brings trouble; the word 'no' leads to no evil.

YOUNG

Everybody has been young before, but not everybody has been old before.

The young are overhanging rocks; the old are trees on the edge of a precipice; no one knows which will fall first.　MADAGASCAR

Youth is beauty, even in cattle.　EGYPT

Teaching in youth is like carving in stone.　MOROCCO

The young cannot teach tradition to the old.　YORUBA

Z

ZEBRA

When you shoot a zebra in the black stripe, the
white dies too; shoot it in the white and the
black dies too.

SOUTH AFRICA

All is never said.
NIGERIA

Everything has an end.
TANZANIA

BIBLIOGRAPHY

R.S. Rattray, Ashanti Proverbs, Oxford University Press, Oxford 1916

William Ernest Taylor, African Aphorisms, Sheldon, London 1924

George Herzog, Jabo Proverbs, Oxford University Press, London 1936

Iet Obenhuijsen, Spiegeltje, Contact, Amsterdam/Antwerpen 1938

C.E.J. Whitting, Hausa and Fulani Proverbs, Lagos 1940

D. Malcolm, Zulu Proverbs, Griggs, Durban 1949

K. ter Laan, Andermans Wijsheid, A.J.G. Strengholt, Amsterdam 1961

Gabriel Pommerand, Le Petit Philosophe de Poche, Le Livre de
    Poche, Parijs 1962

Charlotte en Wolf Leslau, African Proverbs, Peter Pauper Press,
    New York 1962

H. van Roy, Proverbes Congo, Tervuren 1963

W.H. Auden en Louis Kronenberger, The Faber Book of Aphorisms,
    Faber and Faber, London 1964

J.O. Ajibola, Owe Yoruba, Oxford University Press, Ibadan 1971

Achille van Acker, De duivel in spreekwoord en gezegde, Uga,
    Heule 1976

Friedrich Pustet, Wijsheid uit het Oosten, Omega Boek, Amsterdam
    1977

Markus M. Ronner, Neue treffende Pointen, Ott Verlag, Thun 1978

Karl Peltzer en Reinhard von Normann, Das treffende Zitat, Ott
    Verlag, Thun 1979

Edward Westermarck, Wit and wisdom in Morocco, AMS Press,
    New York 1980

Jan Knappert, Namibia, Land and Peoples, Myths and Fables,
    E.J. Brill, Leiden 1981

Ferdinand Walser, Luganda Proverbs, Reimer Verlag, Berlin 1982

Maurice Maloux, Dictionnaire de l'Humour et du Libertinage, Albin
    Michel, Parijs 1984

Isaac Yetiv, 1,001 Proverbs from Tunesia, Three Continents Press,
    Washington, 1987

Gaby Vanden Berghe, Hoofdkussenboekje voor politici, Lannoo,
    Tielt 1988

Daniel Kleinworth, Wijsheid over de natuur, Omega Boek,
    Amsterdam 1988

D.C. Browning, Dictionary of Quotations and Proverbs, Chancellor
    Press, London 1988

Gaby Vanden Berghe, Hoofdkussenboekje voor Verliefden, Lannoo,
    Tielt 1990

Daniel Kleinworth, Liefde voor de natuur, Omega Boek, Amsterdam
1990
Gerd de Ley, Klassiek Citatenboek, Standaard Uitgeverij, Antwerpen
1992
Patricia Houghton, Book of Proverbs, Cassell, London 1992
Lusendi Matukama, Afrikaanse Verhalen en Tradities, C.I.E.E.A.,
Brussels 1993
Roberto Masello, Proverbial Wisdom, Contemporary Books, Chicago
1993
Guy T. Zona, The House of the Heart is never full and other proverbs
of Africa, Simon & Schuster, New York 1993
Gerd de Ley, 1001 Buitenlandse Spreekwoorden, Darbo, Antwerpen
1994
Kathryn & Ross Petras, The Whole World Book of Quotations,
Addison-Wesley Publishing Company, New York 1994
Minneke Schipper, Een vrouw is als de aarde, Afrikaanse
spreekwoorden en zegswijzen over vrouwen, Ambo, Baarn 1994
Gaby Vanden Berghe, Kinderen zijn een brug naar de hemel,
Lannoo, Tielt 1995
Gaby Vanden Berghe, Het ware geluk, gelukkig maken, Lannoo, Tielt
1995
Gaby Vanden Berghe, Wie dankbaar is hoeft niet te blozen, Lannoo,
Tielt 1995
Reginald McKnight, Wisdom of the African World, The Classic
Wisdom Collection, Novato, California 1996
Gerd de Ley, The International Dictionary of Proverbs, Hippocrene
Books, New York 1998
Rainer Crummenerl, Flaschen-Post, Deutsche Seereederei, Rostock
(no year of publication)
Jan Engelman, Adam zelf, Bigot en Van Rossum, Amsterdam
(no year of publication)

INFORMATION

Abyssinia = the old Ethiopia
Akan = tribe in Nigeria
Ashanti = tribe in Ivory Coast
Azande = tribe in Zaire
Bakongo = tribe in Zaire
Bambara = people from the upper regions
of the Niger living in present
day Mali
Bantu = tribe in Southern Africa
Basa = tribe in Liberia & Nigeria
Bemba = tribe in Northern Zimbabwe
Bondei = tribe in Kenya
Buganda = part of Uganda
Chagga = tribe in Tanzania
Dahomey = till November 1975 the name of
the republic Benin, West Africa
Duala = tribe in Cameroon
Efik = tribe in Nigeria
Exe = tribe in Ghana
Fulani = tribe in Cameroon
Fulfulde = tribe in Cameroon
Ga = tribe in Ghana
Galla = tribe in Ethiopia
Gold Coast = now Ghana
Ganda = tribe in Uganda
Guinea = former name of the coastal area
of West and Equatorial Africa
Hausa = tribe in Northern Nigeria
Ho = tribe in Togo
Ibo = tribe in Nigeria
Jabo = tribe in Liberia
Kamba = tribe in Kenya
Kanuri = tribe in Northern Nigeria
Kikuyu = tribe in Kenya
Kru = tribe in Liberia
Kweli = tribe in Cameroon
Malagasy = old name for Madagascar
Masai = tribe in East Africa
Ngone = tribe in Mozambique

Nupe = tribe in Northern Nigeria
Nyang = tribe in Cameroon
Nzima = tribe in Ivory Coast
Oji = tribe in Ivory Coast
Ovambo = tribe in Namibia
Pedi = tribe in South Africa
Peul = people in West Africa
Shona = tribe in South Africa
Sotho = tribe in LeSotho
Swahili = tribe in Kenya
Tamashek = tribe in Central Sahara
Toucouleure = tribe in Mauritania
Tsonga = tribe in Mozambique
Tumbulca = tribe in Malawi
Upper-Volta = Burkino Fasso
Vai = tribe in Liberia & Sierra Leone
Wolof = tribe in Senegal
Xhosa = tribe in Southern Nigeria
Zulu = tribe in South Africa